LETTERS OF FOUR SEASONS

LETTERS OF FOUR SEASONS

Daisaku Ikeda and Yasushi Inoue

Foreword by Burton Watson

Trans. by Richard L. Gage

KODANSHA INTERNATIONAL LTD.
Tokyo, New York & San Francisco

Illustrations by Ikuo Hirayama.

Distributed in the United States by Kodansha International/USA, Ltd. through Harper & Row, Publishers, Inc., 10 East 53rd Street, New York, New York 10022. In South America by Harper & Row, International Dept. In Canada by Fitzhenry & Whiteside Limited, 150 Lesmill Road, Don Mills, Ontario M3B 2T6. In Mexico & Central America by Harla S.A. de C.V., Apartado 30–546, Mexico 4, D.F. In the United Kingdom by Phaidon Press Limited, Littlegate House, St. Ebbe's Street, Oxford OX1 1SQ. In Europe by Boxerbooks, Inc., Limmatstrasse 111, 8031 Zurich. In Australia & New Zealand by Book Wise (Australia) Pty. Ltd., 104–8 Sussex Street, Sydney 2000. In the Far East by Toppan Company (S) Pte. Ltd., No. 38 Liu Fang Road, Jurong Town, Singapore 2262.

Published by Kodansha International Ltd., 2–12–21 Otowa, Bunkyo-ku, Tokyo 112 and Kodansha International/USA, Ltd., 10 East 53rd Street, New York, New York 10022 and 44 Montgomery Street, San Francisco, California 94104. Copyright © 1980 by Daisaku Ikeda and Yasushi Inoue. All rights reserved. Printed in Japan.

LCC 79–91521
ISBN 0–87011–413–1
JBC 0095–787787–2361

First edition, 1980

Foreword

Good letter writing, it has often been noted, is an art. And like most arts, it is governed by fairly strict rules and conventions, though these may vary considerably in nature from one culture to another.

Perhaps because letters are so convention-molded, and because the conventions take such varied forms in different countries, a letter in a foreign language can be a very baffling affair indeed. I recall receiving a letter in Japanese from an acquaintance not long after I first came to Japan as a student. I opened it expecting to find some piece of cheery news from my friend, but instead was confronted with the mysterious announcement: "The sky is high and the horses are fat." I later learned that this is simply one of the conventional "seasonal openings" employed at the beginning of a Japanese letter, this one pertaining to autumn when, because of the clear air, the sky seems to be particularly far away. Japanese etiquette demands that letters and other communications commence with a certain number of platitudinous observations on the season in order to set a relaxed and amiable tone. Once that is over, a special signal word, *sate*, sounds a warning beep and the reader knows that the actual business of the letter is going to begin.

Not only the language of letters but the terms referring to them are often bound up with the usages and history of a culture. The work that follows this Foreword is entitled in Japanese *Shiki no Gansho*, which literally means "Wild Goose Writings of the Four Seasons." To understand the significance of the wild goose, one must know the following story. In the first century B.C., the Chinese emperor sent an envoy to the nomadic tribes living north of China known as the Xiongnu (mentioned on p. 24). The Xiongnu held the envoy in captivity and reported to the Chinese court that he had died, but the Chinese learned of his place of confinement and confronted the Xiongnu with the fact. Asked where they had obtained such information, the Chinese officials replied that a wild goose had been shot down in the emperor's hunting park and that tied to its leg was a letter from the imprisoned envoy. Because of this anecdote, recorded in one of the most famous works of Chinese history, the wild goose has in China and Japan come to be a conventional symbol of letters and letter writing.

Outside of the kind of formulaic salutations and closings I have referred to, there are broader conventions that govern letter writing and make it different from all other literary forms. Since letters in most cases represent an exchange between persons who know each other fairly well and share a common background, they can be much more elliptical than other types of prose, alluding to persons and events without the kind of explanatory material that would ordinarily be required. They can, in other words, be highly compressed and personal in language, and hence a series of riddles to outsiders who are not privy to the facts.

In addition, because they are a form of exchange between persons, they frequently represent an interplay of ideas. A good correspondent not only reports on his own condition and thinking but alludes to the condition and thoughts of the other party as they were reported to him in the letter to which he is replying, commiserating, counseling, agreeing or disagreeing with ideas expressed earlier, or utilizing them to develop a new line of thought. A correspondence is a series of narratives or reflections that two people build together, each taking his turn.

Finally, because the letter is in most cases a rather informal medium of expression, it allows one to ramble from one topic to another. No one expects a letter to state a proposition and develop it step by step to its logical conclusion. To do so would certainly startle the other party in the correspondence and quite possibly offend him. The letter is the ideal medium for trying out new ideas, particularly if one is fortunate enough to have a correspondent who is sympathetic to such novelty, to relate impressions or past happenings just as they come to mind, to be rather irresponsible in utterance and at times perhaps a little incoherent.

The letter is, in short, a highly personal and flexible medium. Its purpose is not so much to convey ideas or facts as it is to convey the living personality of the person who thinks the thoughts and notes the facts. For whatever range of topics may be touched on within it, the real subject of a letter is in the end the writer himself. And we who read the letter do so not so much because we care about what it says as because we care about the person who wrote it.

It may be well to keep these remarks in mind when reading the work that follows, since it consists entirely of a series of letters exchanged between two friends. The correspondents are two men prominent in contemporary Japanese society, Daisaku Ikeda and Yasushi Inoue. Mr. Ikeda was until recently the president of Soka Gakkai, a Buddhist lay organization with a large following in Japan and other countries. At present he holds the position of Soka Gakkai International President. In addition to his activities as a religious and social leader, Mr. Ikeda is a prolific writer of books on Buddhism, essays and poetry; a number of his works have been translated into English. Mr. Inoue is a well-known poet and fiction writer who is particularly noted for his historical novels. One of these, *Tempyō no Iraka*, translated into English by James T. Araki under the title *The Roof Tile of Tempyo* (University of Tokyo Press, 1975), has recently been made into a movie, much of it filmed in China, that is attracting considerable attention at the moment.

In the letters that follow, these two men report to one another on their activities, often relating accounts of travel, since both visited China, Europe and various other places during the period covered. Both men being writers, they comment on their own and one another's works, as well as exchanging thoughts on current issues and more fundamental religious, philosophical and social questions. Here is the kind of give and take of ideas that I have mentioned as being at the heart of good letter writing.

Here too is the relaxed and delightfully rambling approach of a good letter, which moves from reflections on perplexing social problems to descriptions of scenery from a speeding train, delivering comments on one page about Lenin and on another about bush clover. Since the writers share a common cultural background, they refer often to thinkers, artists or other prominent figures in Japanese and Chinese culture. Such references are of course not intended to sound

7

pedantic or obscure, though they may at times seem so to Western readers who do not have the same background. Finally, the letters are sprinkled with the kind of mutual compliments and expressions of polite concern that one would expect of well-bred correspondents. There are even a few amusing examples of overingenious speculation, as when Mr. Inoue opines that Emperor Wu of the Han dynasty located his tomb where he did because he wanted to be near the grave of a favorite general who had died some years earlier. As a matter of fact, chapter six of the *History of the Former Han Dynasty* records that the emperor chose the site of his tomb in 139 B.C., twenty-two years before the death of the general in question. The general was buried where he was so that he would be near the emperor, not the other way around.

These, in sum, are thoughtful and gracefully phrased letters exchanged by men of creative spirit who are leaders in their respective fields of endeavor. Japanese readers would most likely read them because they have an intrinsic interest in the writers themselves. Readers of English, to whom the names of the writers may be less familiar, will no doubt welcome this opportunity to become better acquainted with them.

Burton Watson

Preface

In terms of viewpoint, age and past history, novelist Yasushi Inoue and I are very different. A leading figure in the Japanese literary world, he is profoundly learned in history, on which he turns a clear but warm eye. Though now over seventy years of age, he has traveled the Silk Road, which was once the route of cultural exchange between the Orient and the Occident, and has the passion of a youth for the romance of the regions to the west of China. Recently, he displayed great vigor by accompanying a motion-picture production staff to China, where location work was being done on the filming of his novel, *The Roof Tile of Tempyo*. As he continues to refine his already elegant literary style, he maintains a beautiful, youthful mind and constantly growing will to create that I cannot help respecting.

Our correspondence was conducted for one year, beginning in April, 1975, and the letters were published serially in the Japanese journal *Ushio*. For me, as the person responsible for a large-scale religious movement, this was a busy time in which I remained in no one place very long. For the sake of cultural and educational exchanges and to do my part in the search for peace, I visited China, Europe and the Soviet Union. A believer in Buddhism, the epitome of the wisdom of the Orient, I have profound interest in all human phenomena. For this reason, it was a source of intense happiness for me to correspond with Mr. Inoue and to write him either while traveling or after returning from my journeys.

Each of his letters of the four seasons was rich with literary aroma. Between the lines of the one he wrote while seated at his study window, as balmy May breezes blew, I sensed the energy of the greenery of which he is fond—Mr. Inoue was born in May.

From time to time, among the more casual contents of his letters, he suddenly revealed something about which he had thought deeply or had pondered. Each of these frank revelations floated to the surface as a firmly traced mental image and enlightened me greatly.

In one of my letters to him, I expressed my frank feelings about one of his stories called *Kaseki* (Fossils). Death, the theme of the tale, is a subject that interests me deeply primarily because of its relation to Buddhism, which originates with a clear examination of human life in terms of the Four Sufferings of birth, aging, illness and death and is an exhaustive teaching about the way human beings ought to live. While battling cancer, the hero of Mr. Inoue's story faces and converses with death as a companion. With amazing pride he overcomes his adversary and survives. In our correspondence, Mr. Inoue explained that the background of the story is his own dialogue with the companion death. People today deliberately evade direct confrontations with death. But I believe that they are now beginning introspectively to devote quiet concern to the issue of life and death. For this reason, our letters on this subject left a deep impression on my mind.

The river of time flows mercilessly on, and many different human patterns float to its surface and then disappear. I was to learn of the death of the famous Chinese prime minister Zhou Enlai, whom I had met, during the exchange of letters with Mr. Inoue.

Going beyond the vicissitudes of life, the several open and candid letters we exchanged struck a note of sympathy between us that will not fade. Though the entire correspondence lasted only a year, I am certain its spiritual and philosophical contents have a bearing on the phenomena of modern times.

Though I was somewhat surprised to learn of an English-language edition, as I had been when the letters were first published in book form in Japanese, I consented to the project in the hope that the reader will accept the book for what it is: a milestone in the lives of its authors.

Representing both,

February 16, 1980   Daisaku Ikeda

Teacher and Taught

April 28, 1975

I have just returned from my third trip to China; the first took place in early June and the second at the end of last year. It is now late at night. As I sit writing at my desk, vivid images of the people I met on my sudden trip flash into my mind. I wonder what each of them is doing or thinking. Lost in these reflections, I realize how precious each encounter was and how deep the meaning each has for me is.

The white sunlight of Beijing in April is dazzling. At the time of my last visit to the city, the leafless willow branches were silhouetted against a cold winter sky. Now waves of brilliant light bathed the new green-gold buds, and yellow plum, pink peach and white pear blossoms filled the city streets.

At the pinnacle of this vernal splendor, I was given the unexpected opportunity to meet Prince Norodum Sihanouk of Cambodia. I am told that Sihanouk means lion. And indeed, the prince made an impression of a lion who has suffered and survived long obscurity. Perhaps it was because, only the morning before, word had reached him that Phnom Penh had fallen and that five years of internal strife in his country had come to an end. As is only to be expected, our discussion touched on many lively political topics, but the thing I recall more strongly than what we said were the associations awakened in my mind by a picture, in tones of blue, of Angkor Wat that hung on the wall in the prince's reception room.

Fourteen years earlier, in February, I had visited the ruins of Angkor Wat and had been deeply impressed. The towers, terraces, staircases and mystically smiling faces of the great reliefs suddenly spring up out of their surrounding sea of jungle. The sleeping heritage of the lost Khmer civilization, they seem to have preserved an existence of their own, remote from the rest of human history.

Prince Sihanouk told me that his mother's grave illness prevented his immediate return to Cambodia and added in a subdued voice that, when he did go back, it would be first to Angkor Wat and not to Phnom Penh. Resigned to his mother's imminent death, he intends to travel to the famous ruins to make arrangements for her funeral. With the deep blues of the picture on the wall in my mind, I sympathized with this man, who on the day of victory for his people was forced to grieve for a mother on the verge of death.

Prince Sihanouk spoke of pressures and negotiations among the powerful nations and of his continuing stubborn struggle. "I am used to battle," he said. "No hardship can wear me out." The inflexible faith with which he made this statement revealed him as an outstanding leader filled with resolute intensity. I immediately saw him as a human being who embodies at once the energetic will to struggle and profound human suffering. I felt sure that the people of Cambodia will someday rise up joyously to greet him. But at the moment, the picture of Angkor Wat and thoughts of the prince's dying mother were uppermost in my mind.

Throughout our conversation, his smile reminded me of the expressions on the faces of the Angkor Wat reliefs and of the hope for Cambodian independence that they symbolize. No matter what the vicissitudes of time and history, no matter what hardships and trials they must endure, the people of the nation will be spiritually strengthened by these smiling works of art, which will continue to shed their light on the Cambodian path.

I hope to meet the prince again, but it should be in Angkor Wat, the symbol of the history and culture of his people, rather than Phnom Penh, which is merely a political capital. I hope we do meet and that we can discuss life and friendship as members of the human family, not only as citizens of Cambodia and Japan.

To return to my Chinese trip, this was my first visit to Wuhan. The seventeen hours by train that it takes to get there freshly impressed me with the vastness of the country. From Beijing to Wuhan the scenery hardly changes: red plains stretching far away into the horizon.

Fortunately it was May. I have heard Wuhan is hot enough in the summer to have earned the description, "the city where sparrows fall from the sky of heat exhaustion."

Although the official reason for my visit was to attend presentation ceremonies for a gift of books in Japanese that I made to Wuhan University, I was actually eagerly looking forward to renewing an acquaintance. I met Ms. Wu Yue'e, a teacher of Japanese at the university, the preceding April when she came to Japan for a short stay. The background of our association requires a little explanation.

Two years earlier, a student from Soka University in Tokyo had become a member of a Sino-Japanese friendship group visiting Wuhan University. While there he met Ms. Wu, who as a result came to visit Soka University. At that time, I met her on three occasions. We had dinner together, enjoyed a game of Ping-Pong and played the piano together. And we became good friends.

When I arrived at Wuhan University, a large number of students met our group. In the very front row was Ms. Wu with her three children. We hurried to shake hands and exchange greetings. I was very happy to see her again, for she is a lively, bright and considerate person.

Human contacts on the amicable level of those between Ms. Wu and the student are of the greatest importance to friendship between the Chinese and Japanese peoples and to the safety and security of the whole world. Without a firm basis of natural, friendly exchanges on the individual level, amity on the governmental level is impossible. Each small personal contact is like a drop of water contributing to the formation of a sea of good will.

An excellent example of my meaning is the case of the famous Chinese writer Lu Xun [1881–1936], who studied for a while in Japan. As the only Chinese student at the Sendai Medical Technical School, he lived in surroundings that cannot be described as completely cordial. Lu Xun, with his linguistic handicap to aggravate matters, must have been lonely. One day in autopsy class, however, one of the teachers, a Professor Fujino, instructed Lu to call on him, with his class notes, once a week. From then on, Professor Fujino corrected all of Lu's notes, and Lu never forgot this kindness and the encouragement it gave him. The simple, sincere relation between a lonely foreign student and a college teacher is the model of the kind of relations that I think ought to be carried out on the fullest possible scale. One of Lu's short stories tells of this relation and recalls the Japanese teacher who helped him.

Human contacts like the ones I have been describing are indispensable to revolution, which depends on them if it is to represent the tough human will put into practical action. It is friendship, or comradeship, that moves the minds of men to act in the name of a revolutionary principle, as most of the great struggles that have occurred in the world illustrate. Unity established on a personal basis provides the energy to alter the course of history. Sadly, however, after the revolution has apparently succeeded, unity, comradeship and friendship are often forgotten, with the result that what was formerly a battle for a lofty cause degenerates into a hellish nightmare.

But even unity and comradeship are ineffectual unless they are based on a true sense of the priceless value of human life in its full extension into the worlds of past, present and future. A person who realizes— as we Buddhists do—that his own life extends into these three worlds and is valuable in all of them respects the lives of others. Superficially interpreting life as only something of the present makes harmonious individual encounters on the deepest level difficult.

The best pattern for amicable personal exchanges is the teacher–taught relationship. I am not thinking in the limited terms of the classroom. Nor do I have in mind the relation between master and disciple as advocated by Confucianism, since this is based on authority. I am talking about teaching and being taught on a much broader, richer basis.

Friendly relations are most abundantly fruitful when both parties are simultaneously and mutually teacher and taught. The person who has information in one field should impart it to friends, and they should in their turn be eager to learn. No person is a specialist in all fields and no person is totally ignorant of all fields. Therefore each person is sometimes qualified to be the teacher and sometimes must be the pupil. The process must be, as I have said, mutual and reciprocal. Further, contacts of this kind must transcend ideological and political systems. Though in themselves individual contacts and friendships are modest and limited in scale, they are the only way out of the impasse that political and other jealousies have led mankind into. And as they increase and intensify, they generate universal concern for the welfare of all human beings. This kind of all-inclusive wish to be beneficial to one's fellows is beautifully illustrated in a poem entitled "Autumn wind blew away the thatch" by Du Fu [712–70], one of the greatest Tang-period poets. At one place in the poem occurs the following passage:

> I've slept but little since the days of war.
> How will I last through long, damp, autumn night?
> I long to find a vast and covered hall
> Where all the poor of earth can meet in joy.
> Ah, will I never see it rising tall?

I recalled this poem as I stood on the immense Wuhan Changjiang bridge looking down into the still more immense current of the Yangzi River flowing below.

Daisaku Ikeda

Ochre-stained Hands

May 4, 1975

Sitting in my study, where I enjoy the cool breezes of May, I have spent a refreshing hour reading your letter, learning about your health and sharing some of your impressions of your trip to China. I read in the newspaper of your meeting in Beijing with Prince Sihanouk. I was impressed, but not surprised, to learn that you are the first Japanese citizen to meet him after the liberation of Phnom Penh. I feel certain that, standing at this historic crossroads, at the conclusion of the long internal war that has torn his nation asunder, this bold Cambodian leader found the thoughts of a freethinker like youself, who values individual human contacts, most trustworthy and appealing.

Ceremonies for the presentation of books to Wuhan University were also mentioned in the newspapers. It is easy to talk of them as mere cultural exchange, but actually implementing programs like this is not easy. Such a large gift of books—three thousand volumes, I believe—in the Japanese language is certain to bear fruit in future friendly relations between China and Japan. I was very happy to learn that some of my own works are among the books presented.

I read with great interest and sympathy the cases of human contacts you relate: the one between Ms. Wu of Wuhan University and the Japanese student, and the one between Lu Xun and his Japanese teacher, Professor Fujino. I too firmly believe that relations among nations must begin with individual exchanges and not with political or nationalistic attitudes. Some people hold that politics must be cooly detached from human emotions, but as long as it deals with human beings, politics must take feelings into consideration. Political philosophies that

16

fail to do so contribute nothing to the discovery of solutions for the current world confusion.

Last fall, while an exhibition of Han and Tang murals was being held here, Wang Yeqiu, director of the Chinese National Bureau of Cultural Undertakings and noted research expert on ancient Chinese civilization, visited this country. Whenever I am in China, he is always most helpful in guiding me through the Palace Museum and showing me things I especially want to see. At each meeting, I am more deeply impressed by his learning and his warm sincerity. When I met him shortly after his arrival in Tokyo on this occasion, I found I had not been the first person he called on. As might have been expected, he went first to an archaeologist, Professor Shukujin Harada. Mr. Wang returned to China not long after that, and a few days later, I was oddly saddened to read in the newspaper of the death of Professor Harada. Mr. Wang was probably the last foreign scholar to see the professor, and I was glad that they had had this final opportunity. This is all there is to the incident, and though I knew neither of them well, I was moved to learn of a friendship between two men based solely on the love of learning.

I do have one other thing to relate about Mr. Wang, however. On the occasion of the visit during which he met Professor Harada, he made a request of me. He told me that he had read in something written by the late Professor Shōnan Naito of the existence in Japan of rubbings taken from memorial stones at the temple Yongning-si, located in Shanxi Province. On the backs of the stones from which the rubbings were made is writing in the languages of the Nüzhen and Qidan Tartars, and Mr. Wang was interested in obtaining photographs or copies of them.

Our conversation was carried out with the help of interpreters. I am not a specialist in these matters and had no idea where such rubbings might be found. No good ideas for finding them came to me at the moment. Nonetheless, I promised to do what I could to be of assistance. About two months later, as the end of the year drew near, at a publisher's party, I met Toshio Nagahiro, a professor emeritus at Kyoto University. Suddenly remembering Mr. Wang's request, I mentioned the Yongning-si rubbings to him. He said he too was in Mr. Wang's debt for kindnesses and would like to try to repay him by undertaking the search for the rubbings. He then explained to me why he was obliged to Mr. Wang.

"About ten years ago, before relations between China and Japan were normalized, Mr. Wang visited this country as the head of a group in charge of holding an exhibition of murals from the Yongle Palace. I feel sure this was his first visit to Japan. Mr. Wang was guided through Nara, and at a dinner at the Nara Hotel I mentioned the lack in Japan of original rubbings from the Yongning-si stone murals. The dinner took place in October. At the end of the same year, someone brought eighty rubbings of these stones from Wang Yeqiu. Though not suspecting that a casual remark made at dinner would produce such results in such a hurry, I was delighted at the good will of a man who could do such an unheard of thing when there were still no formal relations between the two nations involved. Those rubbings are now preserved in the Research Institute for Humanistic Studies of Kyoto University."

This was the reason Mr. Nagahiro was eager to do something for this Chinese scholar who had demonstrated such good faith and sincerity. Two or three days ago, a number of photographs of the rubbings Mr. Wang wants arrived here. They are in my possession at present.

On May 8, with a group of Japanese writers, I am invited to visit China. While there, I shall relate to Mr. Wang Professor Nagahiro's long-sustained gratitude and shall hand to him personally the photographs of the Yongning-si rubbings. I consider this story a fine example of the kind of exchange that you wish to inspire and of the good that can come of warm human concern. Cultural exchanges among nations must come about through such personal encounters, as has often been the case in the past.

You said you traveled by train from Beijing to Wuhan. As a matter of fact, twenty years ago, once again as a member of a group of Japanese writers, I traveled the same route but in the opposite direction, that is, I went by train from Guangzhou to Wuhan and from there to Beijing. I too was impressed for the first time by the size of China and had a chance to see the Yangzi at the great Wuhan Bridge. I am told that the appearance and current of the river change from season to season. When I saw it, the energy of the flow and the amount of yellow earth it was moving struck me as being at a peak. The river assumed a different significance when, standing on the bank, I saw a group of women washing large jugs in its waters. Little human lives are still being lived beside this ever-flowing river just as they were centuries ago. I at once perceived something eternal in the Yangzi. And I can never think of its torrent of earth-yellowed water in my old way again. For countless ages, human beings have acted and the river has flowed side by side.

As I watched women turning their hands red-ochre by washing jugs in the cold, eternal Yangzi, I too wanted to come in touch with the harsh facts of cold reality as they were. As a writer, I wanted to come into contact with the everlasting, as those women do. Believing in eternity, in humanity, and in the society humanity can build, like the Chinese women washing jugs and reddening their hands in the water, I want to color my hands with real experience through my work.

From the window of my study, I can look out on my small garden, where azaleas, peonies, wild yellow roses and bridal wreath are blooming under an enveloping canopy of green trees rustling in the thrilling energy of a high May wind. I like the month of May, but not only because I was born on the sixth day. I like the darkness of its mountains and the luminescence of its fair skies. The mountains at this time of year are vibrantly alive. In May, gloom is deeper and brilliance more

dazzling. May rains fall as if very serious about their work, and the blue May sky looks eternally fresh and clean—especially when colorful carp streamers for Boys' Day fly against it.

Not just my May, but everybody's birth month has its good points. We only have to look for them. Some of my friends laugh at me for being proud of May, but I suspect that it is important to feel this way, just as it is important to be proud of the country in which one was born. As long as Japan is the land of one's birth, it is good to try to discover what is good about it and to cultivate and be proud of these things. This morning I saw another of the currently faddish negative articles about Japanese culture and history that turn up in the journalistic media with some frequency. My reaction against articles of this kind has inspired me to make these comments.

I hear that you are to go to Europe soon. I hope you have a safe journey.

Yasushi Inoue

The Emperor and His Warrior

June 12, 1975

I received your last letter in May, just before I left on a three-week trip to China, from which I have just returned and about which I should like to tell you. Although I came back at the end of last month, I have been staying close to home for about a week, as is my habit after a journey. Usually I spend the time sitting in a wicker chair on the veranda adjacent to my study, doing nothing but putting my travel diary in order. The heavy oppressive rainy season had already set in, and I have been generally idle. With the master gone for a while, the garden has run wild. Of course a bare month's absence does not actually make that much difference, still it looks overrun to me. The roses in their little beds have grown straggly, the white star lilies have gotten out of hand, and weeds choke the lawn. But sitting here looking out at the unruly plot, thinking over the time I have recently spent elsewhere, is necessary. The trip is over, but it lingers. I need a chance to look things up, to deepen, correct and amplify my impressions.

We started in Beijing, went to Luoyang, Xi'an, Yan'an and then to Beijing again. Then we traveled to Wuxi and Shanghai, returning a final time to Beijing before flying to Tokyo. On this final occasion, I met Wang Yeqiu and gave him the stone rubbings from the Yong-ning-si temple, which, as I told you in an earlier letter, had been entrusted to me by Toshio Nagahiro. I was happy to play the part of mediator in a learned exchange between Japanese and Chinese archaeologists.

Mr. Wang, who was very happy to have the rubbings, held a dinner for us Japanese writers and critics, and we spent some of our precious

time discussing the Datung and Lungmen caves, the Great and Small Gander pagodas of Xi'an, and the Hōryū-ji and Yakushi-ji temples.

Owing to some unfinished business, I have interrupted the writing of this letter for a few days. During that time, I read in the newspaper that you recently finished a busy and significant tour of Paris, London and Moscow, where you not only lectured at the University of Moscow but also received an honorary doctorate. In perusing the full text of your message, "The New Way to Cultural Exchanges between East and West," I was, among other things, especially interested by your highly meaningful term the "Silk Road of the Spirit" and by your insistence that cultural exchanges must be imbued with a sense of equality and mutual understanding. Since I am certain that in the future I will have an opportunity to hear more from you on these topics and to express my own opinions of them, I will say here only that I am happy you have completed a fruitful journey and have come home in good health.

To return to my own Chinese trip, I should like to share with you one or two of the impressions made on me by the ancient cities Luoyang and Xi'an. I had already visited Xi'an once, twelve years ago, but this was my first time in Luoyang. Obviously I wanted to see the famous Lungmen caves, but I was even more interested to know precisely where in the modern city Luoyang, the capital of the Eastern Zhou, is located. It is as this capital that Luoyang first appears in history.

"Where is the site of the walled city of the Eastern Zhou?" This question I prepared before leaving Tokyo and popped on one of the guides showing us around the city and its environs on the very day of our arrival. Finally, our driver stopped in a place outside the modern city and said, "This is said to be the location of Luoyang as it was in the Eastern Zhou period, but today there is a laborers' park on top of it."

In the neighborhood are a number of new factories and large apartment buildings for the workers. The area could be described as both industrial and residential. We did not go into the park, but I could see a fine stand of trees beneath which slumbers the city that flourished in the third and second centuries B.C. The steps taken in connection with the site of the ruins seemed correct to me. It is not part of the residential area, nor has the industrial belt encroached upon it. Putting a park on the land is an excellent idea. When the time comes, excavations can be carried out with relative ease. Until then, the ruins are completely protected, and the people of the modern city have a pleasant place to relax. Of course, such a thing is possible only in a nation as vast as China and would be out of the question in the case of such places of archaeological interest as Nara and Asuka in Japan. Nonetheless, it is a clever and wise procedure to adopt.

At Xi'an, on the northwest outskirts of the city, we viewed the Mao-ling burial mound of the Han emperor Wu [reigned from 141 to 87 B.C.] and that of the general Huo Qubing located not far away. I suspect we foreigners were permitted to look at these mounds because they have recently been designated important national cultural properties.

The mounds are actually nothing more than apparently ordinary hills in the middle of a flat plain, but the one for the emperor Wu is sizable (46.5 meters high and 240 meters around at the base). At one side of the mound for Huo Qubing is a museum for documents and the sixteen huge pieces of stone sculpture that once stood on the periphery of the memorial hill itself.

I was deeply moved by the two mounds raised in a plain two thousand years ago in memory of an autocrat and one of his outstanding retainers. Since I have written about the time of the Han emperor Wu in other of my books, I do not need to linger on the subject here. Huo Qubing, however, deserves a few words of explanation as the flower of the most glorious part of his master's reign. This was the time when the incursions of the barbarian Xiongnu (probably the Huns) were stopped and, after a number of campaigns, the Xiongnu themselves were conquered.

Of lowly background, Huo entered the service of the emperor at a young age and, by the time he was eighteen, was leading an army of eight hundred cavalry in a brilliant war. Later, in six other campaigns involving tens of thousands of soldiers, he led the emperor's armies and drove the Xiongnu out of Gansu, thus opening a way to the Western Regions. But Huo Qubing died of illness at the age of twenty-four, about thirty years before the emperor. Wu was probably never blessed with this young man's likes again.

I suspect that, in late years, when deciding on the site for his own burial mound, the emperor wanted it to be close to that of his long-dead young general. Huo's mound is not large (14–15 meters high) but is said to have been made in the shape of the mountain Qilian-shan, where the young general often waged war successfully. Furthermore, the sculpture, now on display in the museum but once standing at the foot of the mound, is thought to be made of stone brought from that same mountain. I want to believe that both of these traditions are true.

I saw the stone sculpture this time and was surprised by its excellence. The subject matter ranges from fish, horses, cows, boars, frogs and wailing human beings to monsters eating bleating sheep, running horses, kneeling horses, and horses trampling on Xiongnu. The forms and qualities of the natural stone are fully employed to produce striking physical and psychological effects. Made in praise of the martial glory of Huo and in honor of his spirit, these statues have a delicacy and power that make them masterpieces of Han-period stone sculpture.

Throughout my trip, the idea of the two burial mounds stayed with me. From time to time, their images flashed on my inner eye, as if I ought to have definite thoughts about what they represent. But it was not until I returned to Japan that I discovered the source of the powerful effect they had on me. I believe it was the uncalculated, true affection that bound together the mighty autocrat and his faithful warrior and is symbolized in the proximity of their tombs.

Undeniably the emperor Wu was an outstanding politician and ruler, but the facts of the untimely deaths of his consort Zhen and of Gouyi show that he was hardboiled and difficult as well. While recognizing his many positive traits, historians today cannot ignore the negative ones, which contributed to a veritable explosion of agrarian insurrections that plagued the last part of his reign. Nonetheless, the emperor's love for his young warrior reveals his best aspects. As he approached seventy, the old ruler must have experienced deep, powerful affection for the memory of the general who had been his mainstay in the bright, glorious years. And this love must have been a spot of light in the darkness gathering around him.

I have written several works on subjects related to the Han emperor Wu but never appreciated his better side until this trip. Some people may accuse me of reading too much into the mere placement of the two burial mounds. But this is my interpretation, and I intend to stick by it.

During my second stay in Beijing, I received the shocking news that my friend the writer Shōgo Nomura had died. He visited me only about two weeks before my departure. We discussed plans for his future work for an hour, and I had no idea anything serious enough to take him away was wrong. For a while after I received word, I could not believe it had happened.

He and I had worked together on the newspaper *Mainichi Shimbun* when we were young and had both begun writing novels at about the same time. In the early stage, when I was feverishly trying to become independent, he often covered up for me at the newspaper by doing work that was my duty. Because of him, I was able to get a good start. It was as if he stood aside at the most important time and said kindly, "You go ahead first." At any rate, the attitude summed up in those words often seemed to be in his eyes. As a matter of fact, he did move into an active literary life later than I and did subtle, refined work. Just at the point when his qualities were about to bear their finest fruit, death took him. Hearing the news, I had the haunting suspicion that something that should have been said between us was left unsaid. I ought to have told this best of friends, this benefactor, something. But the unsaid is forever silent; it is left behind with me.

That night, after midnight, I looked down on the city from the balcony of my room in the Beijing Hotel. No cars, no people were on the freshly washed expanse of Chang'an Boulevard below. The huge street lamps on either side illuminated silence and stillness. I felt as if all Beijing were in mourning for my lost, dear friend. And, speaking to myself, I told him so.

Yasushi Inoue

Revolutions

The oppressiveness of the rainy season is especially hard to bear this morning. I suppose your trip to China, the events before and after, and my own trip to the Soviet Union have kept us so busy that we have not yet fully recovered. Maybe it is my own impatient personality, but since returning to Japan, I have been unable to settle down. Your letter dispelled some of the heaviness of the summer air and calmed me. I was especially impressed by what you have to say about the burial mounds of the Han emperor Wu and his general Huo Qubing. Though, unfortunately, I have never visited that part of China, your writing gives me a very vivid idea of what it is like.

Tacitly historical ruins inspire a deep sense of significance. Your perspicacious eye for history has brought new life to the drama of affection between the emperor and his warrior. Throughout life, we have many opportunities to meet many different persons, but the friends who stay by our sides in the darkest, as well as the brightest, hours are most valuable. I can fully believe in what you describe as the strong love the elderly emperor felt for the young general who, after serving him well, died an untimely death. Your personal comments on the loss of your dear friend inspired profound sympathy in me.

In an earlier letter you remarked on a fondness for the month of May. I share your fondness, and for some reason, many of my trips to Europe take place at that time of the year. This year, too, I enjoyed the fresh budding May greenery in Paris, London and Moscow. Paris was especially pleasant. The chestnut trees were covered with white flowers, the petals of which fell to star the black pavement. Gentle sunlight fell on the rippling waters of the warming Seine to harmonize with the historical monuments of this inexhaustibly attractive city.

More attractive still were the chances I had to meet and exchange opinions with people. I enjoyed second meetings with André Malraux, René Huyghe and Giles Martinet and a first meeting with Aurelio Peccei, the director and founder of the Club of Rome, who, as you may know, came to Tokyo for a general meeting of that club two years ago. As is clear from their controversial report, "Limitations of Growth," the members of the Club of Rome are warning mankind about the dangers of the future and are trying to find solutions to some of humanity's gravest problems. Mr. Peccei, who says that material development has reached its limits, advocates a human revolution.

Our civilization already faces crises in connection with natural resources, foodstuffs and population increases. But Mr. Peccei believes in human possibilities and in man's wisdom to make the correct new choices and adaptations. This belief is the foundation of his insistence on a humanistic revolution within the hearts of men. He says that the three major revolutions of human history—industrial, scientific and technological—have all been external and are the ultimate causes of the confusion and danger of our times. Adding that today a revolution in the minds of men is utterly essential, Peccei acts in full confidence that humanity is capable of such revolution. Laughingly commenting that he is optimistic by nature, he impresses me as a true idealist ready to undergo hardships and to make whatever challenges are necessary for future development in the right direction. During our conversation, I could not help wondering what the source of his determination is.

I learned that he had at one time been imprisoned, as I once was and as my mentor Jōsei Toda and his teacher Tsunesaburō Makiguchi were, during World War II, for the unrelenting strength of their religious convictions. With some personal knowledge of its effects, I suspected that Mr. Peccei's own imprisonment for battling with the Fascist authorities gave him determination and strength and inspired him to act as he does. It seemed to me that when talking about his term in prison, Mr. Peccei, who is generally soft-mannered, though physically and mentally powerful, allowed a sudden fierce light to flash in his eyes for an instant, as if he were struggling with old memories.

In 1943, when Hitler and Mussolini fanned the flames of Fascism and they roared throughout Europe, Mr. Peccei was working in the Fiat factory and at the same time taking part in the largest of all Italian underground resistance movements. That year he finished a secret mission in Rome and returned to Turin. Ordinarily he took care to avoid appearing in public places where he might be recognized. But, for some reason, on a certain day he went into a restaurant, was met by a patrolling inspector who discovered the resistance documents he was carrying and was arrested on the spot. He now says that at first everything in prison was unbearable, especially for people like him who belonged to the most mercilessly hated class of political offenders. He repeatedly and for long periods suffered torture. Though prepared to die many times, he never gave in. A friend who had acted as his guarantor and lawyer was also tortured time and time again but refused to incriminate Mr. Peccei, who at last, thanks to this man's courageous behavior, was released. As he spoke of this friend, I saw unfathomable gratitude in his eyes.

During the year he spent in prison, he came, for the first time in his life, to understand the meaning of his own existence. To escape from incessant anxiety, he could do nothing but think of the future. This saved him from the present and inspired him with the determination to devote himself to working for the sake of all society when he was once again free.

After the end of the war, as an industrialist, he helped to rebuild the Italian economy. In addition, in his extensive business travels to many parts of the world, he came face to face with the poverty and distress of the underdeveloped regions. These experiences awakened him to the crises awaiting mankind in the future unless something revolutionary is done at once. And ultimately these events and his reactions to them led him to found the Club of Rome.

He has forgiven the people who persecuted him and from the well of extreme bitterness of his earlier life has drawn concern for the future and the will to act to do something about it. I think this is admirable. From my talks with Mr. Peccei, I became deeply convinced that, though it is important to resist all kinds of oppression, the best way to ensure resistance is to cultivate knowledge and pride in the ordinary people to such an extent that they will be unable to tolerate unfair pressures from above. It is equally important to educate holders of power to their duties in connection with the well being of humanity and to help them avoid the evils latent in positions of privilege and authority.

My meeting with Aurelio Peccei came about as a consequence of the two years of dialogues conducted by the late Arnold J. Toynbee and me. At the conclusion of our series of talks, Mr. Toynbee gave me a list of seven people he thought it would be advantageous for me to meet, and Mr. Peccei was one of them.

Spring was at its peak when I was in Moscow on this trip. Though we had occasional cool days, generally the weather was warm enough for shirtsleeves. The dandelionlike white blossoms of the poplar trees were blowing and dancing in the air. The purpose of my trip to the Soviet Union was cultural and educational exchange. As you kindly noted, I did deliver a message at Moscow University—thank you for taking time to read it in the newspaper—and I did receive an honorary doctorate. But I put very little importance on things of that kind in these troubled times. I prefer not to be known by titles but as a traveler on the Silk Road of the Spirit, doing what he can to unite the hearts and minds of as many people as is possible.

While in Moscow, I visited Gorki-Leninskie, where Lenin spent his last months and where he died. The building in which he was cared for is on the outskirts in a very Russian-looking, tree-surrounded place. It is said that when he was stricken with his fatal illness, he continued his long, hard battle for the revolution by planning and thinking about the future of the new nation. As I walked through the groves around Gorki-Leninskie, which is now a carefully protected museum, the birch trees seemed engulfed in the sea of sunlight washing around, over and through them. In 1923, the year before Lenin's death, a group of workers from a nearby factory came to pay their respects and planted eighteen cherry trees where they would be visible from his bedroom window. Workers of the same factory have cared for them all this time, and the trees were bearing early fruit when I saw them.

In the museum in the house are letters from children all over the country who were concerned about Lenin's health. One word about this man spelled happiness or sorrow for all of Russia. Some of the letters were addressed to Auntie Krupskaya, Lenin's wife, and requested her to take good care of her husband, since news of his recovery would bring happiness to the whole world. Observing this evidence of devotion gave me a clear conception of the way Lenin's own love of humanity and of his people has rebounded in the affection for him that has survived the siftings of time to be handed down from generation to generation and even to the present.

An especially striking illustration of this is the sculpture group of soldiers and peasants, sorrowfully leaning slightly forward as, in their deep grief and loss, they bear Lenin's body. The statues, which are the work of the artist who took Lenin's death mask, are buried in floral tributes from devoted Russian citizens. The expressions on the faces of the statues and the strength depicted in the way they tread the ground symbolize the will of the ordinary people to withstand the grief of their loss, to look forward to the future and the fulfillment of his will.

I believe that, removed from the smell of politics and placed in the context of the simple, direct emotions of the people, the slogan "Lenin lived, lives today and will live forever" can help us understand Lenin as a vibrant individual human being.

Daisaku Ikeda

Learning from Youth

July 11, 1975

Though the rainy season promises to break soon and we are beginning to see a little more blue sky, the heat is still oppressive. I hope you are bearing up well. For about a week, at the invitation of Soka University, I have been staying here at the campus in Hachioji to attend the Takiyama festival, which was held on July 5 and 6, just before the Tanabata Festival of the Stars, under the sponsorship of the students of the university's Takiyama dormitory. Soka University is still young, and I am happy to see the students rapidly creating a tradition of their own by means of celebrations of this kind. A week's stay in one place for a person who moves around as much as I do has given me an excellent opportunity to come into contact with many young people.

The neighborhood of the campus is gradually being urbanized, but from place to place there still remain traces of the woodland scenery for which this Musashi area was once famous. There is a great deal of bush clover in the vicinity, and the university has recently opened a small garden filled with this autumn-blooming plant. Right now the space is filled with beautiful deep purple iris stretching away toward the profound green of the distant hills. I visited the garden, however, in honor of the bush clover, for I am very fond of it and the way it blooms in a charming profusion of pink and white flowers that indicate strength in delicacy. I regard this humble flowering plant as a symbol of the life of cultured peace and am happy to recall the people of ancient Japan, who in the age when the poems in the collection called *Manyōshū* were being written used bush clover as a hair ornament.

Not far from the garden are dark places said to be infested with snakes. Obviously the beauty of the world of nature depends on the balance between darks and lights, but I believe students and all young people—indeed all people—should spend their time in the bright clover gardens of life and not in the gloomy swamplands. They should find strength to face the challenges before them in the gold of sunlight and the silver of moon and stars.

The biggest attraction at the Takiyama festival were pieces of space equipment lent by the Soviet Union as a return gesture of good will for my trip to Moscow. On display were the satellite Sputnik 1, the first unmanned spacecraft to land on the moon and the liquid-fuel rocket that puts satellites in space. While looking at this popular exhibition, I suddenly thought of the Soyuz-Apollo docking, which is supposed to take place soon between Soviet and American spacecraft. It is said that when American and Soviet forces met at the Elbe in their joint drive against the Nazis, they shook hands enthusiastically as a symbol of the friendship between their two nations. The men on board the two docking spacecraft will no doubt shake hands. I hope this time it will stand for more than amity between nations. I hope it will represent sincere good will for all peoples everywhere.

Standing in front of the not very large machine that had traveled to and returned from the moon, besides amazement at modern technical skills, I experienced a mystical feeling. We may now be deprived of old romantic tales of men—or rabbits, in the Japanese version—in the moon, but science is opening the way for new romances to take the place of the old ones.

I read all of the poems in your collection *Kitaguni* (North Country) with great interest, though one of them named "Shikkoson" appealed to me especially strongly. The poem was about the tranquility an exhibition of the ancient treasures from the Shōsōin repository had on the war-weary population of Japan shortly after World War II. In the poem you compare "Shikkoson," an ancient lacquered vessel, to a meteorite falling through the skies for thousands of years. There might seem to be no direct relation between this poem and the display of Soviet space equipment at the Takiyama festival. In fact, however, the effect ancient things like the Shōsōin treasures and the lacquer container have on people today inspired me to wonder what people of the remote future will think if they have a chance to examine the things on display at the university now. I hope they will be able to see in them a monument to a universal improvement in human behavior. I hope these—by that time—weird and primitive pieces of equipment will stand for the turning point at which mankind ceased torturing itself and ruining its surroundings.

Whenever I am with young people, as I was a great deal during the festival, I sense the presence of my late teacher and mentor Jōsei Toda by my side and can almost see him as he was whenever he conversed with the young.

Every human being has a day, or several days, of special importance to him. July 3 is such a day for me. On that day, in 1945, not long before the end of World War II, my teacher Jōsei Toda was released from the prison cell to which he had been confined by the Japanese military government. His only crime was his religious beliefs.

I first met Jōsei Toda when I was a nineteen-year-old boy trying hard to make sense of life in postwar Japan. Because of that meeting, my becoming a Buddhist and the entire subsequent course of my life were decided. With receding hair and thick glasses, as he puffed on a cigarette, Mr. Toda asked me my age. Though at the time I was uninterested in Buddhism and in religion in general, subconsciously I was searching for someone to be my mentor in life. After asking Mr. Toda a few questions and after learning he had been brave enough to resist the senseless war and the militarists and had not been afraid to go to prison for what he believed, I realized that he was a man I could follow wholeheartedly.

Though he suffered probably as much as Aurelio Peccei, whose experiences I mentioned in a previous letter, while in his cell, Jōsei Toda was more intensely concerned for his teacher Tsunesaburō Makiguchi than he was for himself. Makiguchi had been imprisoned at the same time as Toda for the same reasons. And in spite of his advanced age, he was kept in solitary confinement. When informed offhandedly that "Makiguchi is dead," the usually manful Toda wept. In later years, he used to say, "Mr. Makiguchi permitted me to go to prison with him." From these unexpected words, I understood that, at the time of the announcement of Makiguchi's death, Toda determined to spend the rest of his life following in his master's footsteps.

This is the thirtieth anniversary of Jōsei Toda's release from prison, and on the third of July, just before coming here to the university, a number of his other students and I held a gathering to commemorate the occasion. His wife and son attended and we all shared old experiences together as we renewed our vows to carry on the work he started.

Things did not always go as Jōsei Toda hoped. After his release from prison and the termination of the war, he set out to succeed in business in order to ensure a firm basis for the reconstruction of Soka Gakkai. Frustrations were so frequent that he barely noted the changing of the seasons. I recall one evening when another plan to get us out of our difficulties had failed, he and I were walking along a dark street. At the time a song with the words "Who made me the woman I am?" was popular. You may remember it. At any rate, as we walked, I sang, "Who made me the man I am?" Turning to look at me, he said, "I did."

In a very real sense this is true. Deeply touched by the warmth that inspired him to say this and the affection he showed even when being strict with me, I vowed to be true to him and his teachings always.

Jōsei Toda was an unbridled man. He appeared in front of people in the most informal attire. He liked to drink and to tell jokes that set his companions guffawing. But on the basis of this kind of behavior alone, he is impossible to understand. There was much more to him.

My aim was to learn the optimum way to live from him, and day by day, walking by his side, I poured all my youthful vigor into this learning process. I first learned about Buddhism from Jōsei Toda. Faith did not come first; my encounter with him did. Faith came later.

I am explaining this now because I believe that, just as humanity in the form of Jōsei Toda was the detonating element in my relation with Buddhism, so humanity and concern for its well being should be the starting point of everything in society. Humanity is the great axis. A society in which authority takes precedence over it is not an admirable society. Only when humanity itself is given the place of preeminence is it possible to make a meaningful breakthrough in our search for solutions to the problems of our age and the apathy plaguing human relations today.

Refusing to bow to authority, Jōsei Toda was the ally of the poor and suffering. He was happiest going from house to house mixing with ordinary people and discussing their hardships. He was especially fond of young people, in whom he saw the strength to build the new age.

Indeed, closeness to the ordinary people and love of youth were the two definitive elements of his personality. He knew that people of more advanced years have much to learn from the purity and vigor of the young.

He died in 1957 but has continued to live in my heart where he sometimes keeps silent watch on what I do and sometimes wordlessly gives me counsel. Our lives have coalesced. We breathe together.

Daisaku Ikeda

Starting from Scratch

From what the newspapers relate about some of your activities, you are indeed a busy man. Just as I was beginning to be concerned about you as I would be for a close friend, I received your letter, which was completely refreshing and gives no hint of your hectic schedule. I am very pleased.

Perhaps inspired by your vigorous activity, this year I am breaking with my usual custom of traveling to my small workplace in the cool mountain retreat of Karuizawa at the beginning of July and intend to brave the Tokyo summer. I have made the decision to stay here to finish a piece of work requiring that I be near my library.

I have no detailed information on the Takiyama festival, but your words paint a vivid picture of the proceedings and hint at the encounters you had with young minds. Whenever I am with my own children, I think of young people as fountains, unsullied, inexhaustible fountains of possibilities. Though I cannot say in what direction or how the fountains will flow in the future, right now they bubble pure and clean and are both dazzling and a little frightening.

It is a wonderful thing for you and for them that you have an opportunity to come into close mental contact with young people often. You must draw the extraordinary energy for your active life from such encounters. I suspect youth is a source of basic material for both your reflective thought and your enthusiastic ideals.

You mention the opening of a small bush-clover garden near the campus. I share your fondness for this charming, gentle plant and its exceptional pink and white blossoms. In a corner of the plot at my workplace in Karuizawa, a few clumps of it have come up all on their own. When the number of tourists dwindles and the clamor of the season dies down, these plants, as if deliberately choosing the time of year, bloom to show their small lives to full advantage. Mention is made of a plant that is probably bush clover in a poem by Bai Zuyi [772–864], though in the vicinity of Chang'an, the capital of the Tang dynasty when this poet lived, the plant blooms much later than it does here in Japan.

Your comment about the use of the flowers as hair ornaments by the people at the time of the *Manyōshū* reminds me of two projects I want to carry out, but as of yet have not. One is to glean all the mentions of bush clover in that poetry collection and in other ancient Japanese poetry. The other is to visit the small white-gravel garden in the Kyoto Imperial Palace that is ornamented with nothing but bush clover and must produce a powerful feeling of the distant past.

Like you, I have complicated reactions to highly sophisticated technological equipment like that on display at Soka University through the good offices of the Soviet government and to such things as the recent, successful docking between the Soyuz and Apollo craft. Since I have only seen the things you describe in photographs, I can form no definite opinions about them. But we must all pray that somewhere they include a seat for a kind of divine justice that is deeply interested in the happiness of mankind.

Much has happened to change our attitude toward the heavens. When I was still in senior high school, a friend taught me some words from Immanuel Kant's *Critique of Pure Reason*: "No matter how I try, I can never cease wondering at the stars glittering in the heavens and at the moral law within myself." I am not certain that these were my friend's exact words and can no longer verify them, since he is dead. But this is the form in which the idea has been lodged in my mind for years, together with an image of my friend's face.

Last year, I checked in a Japanese translation of Kant to find out what the correct quotation is. "The more often and the longer I think of them, there are two things that cause my heart increasingly new and greater reverence and wonder: the sky glittering with stars above me and the moral law within me."

My friend abbreviated and simplified, he may even have been a little mistaken, but the impressions I get from the two versions are roughly the same. "No matter how I try, I can never cease wondering at the stars glittering in the heavens and the moral law within myself." This is good enough for me.

I was a physics student with no knowledge worthy of the name and with no understanding of Kant or philosophy of any kind, but my friend's brief version of the philosopher's idea took a lasting hold on my mind. This did not inspire me to read Kant or to try to gain deeper understanding of the words; the words themselves sufficed.

In the heavens the mysterious stars sparkle; on earth, even in suffering, human beings try to live the right way. This is only my own, self-styled, literary interpretation of the passage. When young, I knew many other excellent phrases, but none of them were as impressive as this. No others exerted a controlling influence on me for such a long time. Because of this, I came to understand the mystical night sky as beautiful. And I was able to convince myself that the act of living is valuable in itself. My friend's version of Kant appealed so strongly that, in my youth, the words gave me courage to live.

Now I find it difficult to present these words to young people in a way that is appealing. Youth finds the glittering heavens, the star-jeweled night sky less mysterious. The amazing progress of modern science has subjugated the mystery of heaven. It has carried people to the moon and has brought them back again. As you say, the romance of the folk-tale rabbit in the moon has already lost its luster and is likely to fade still more. You seem to think, or want to believe, that new romances will emerge to take the place of the old ones. Perhaps the moon craft that ripped the old magic away from earth's satellite will become an object of romantic musings on the part of people of the distant future. I hope that new fairy tales will be born and that they are infinitely brighter and happier than anything we can imagine today. I hope they are filled with the joy of living. And if, as I said earlier, these sophisticated spacecraft, around which future folklore will be woven, include a seat for divine justice, the moon can be a luminous colony for all mankind, not for some specific nations alone. In the twentieth century man has violated the mystery of the moon, and it is his responsibility and that of the science he has created to ensure that there is a place for such a divinity.

"No matter how I try, I can never cease wondering at the stars glittering in the heavens and the moral law within myself." But the stars glittering in the heavens are not the same for young people today as they were for me in my youth. And the moral law, the positive understanding of the self and of humanity that was in my heart, is not the same as the things that are in their hearts now. All over the world, philosophical absolutes and religious divinities are weakening, and nothing new is coming into being to take their places. For a while, after the end of World War II, it looked as if human love might fit the bill. But all too soon the unattractive side of this emotion came to the forefront. Young people in postwar Japan were cast on a field of desolation from which all the older value systems had been blasted. It was only natural that they make a fresh start by questioning first principles. They had to reexamine such basic things as the nature of humanity, living, parenthood and parent-child relations from scratch. In the face of this questioning youth, the older generations have remained powerless. And this situation has produced the apparently unresolvable disorder reigning in much of society.

Fundamentally, I was not very different from contemporary youth today. I too got carried away with futile actions. I longed to devote my life to something valuable with a fervor that would consume my being. Young people today probably feel the same way. But in our time we were not left to ourselves as they are. All of us believed in some kind of god. We believed in a scholar or in scholarship itself; we believed that right actually exists. All that kind of thing has been swept away, and philosophy, religion and morality must be created anew, from the ground up. Of course, the effort to bring this about has been the central element in the fervent work you have carried out for a long time.

Yasushi Inoue

Days Aflame

In spite of the heat, I have been in Tokyo throughout July and now, halfway through August, am glancing through the newspaper—dated the first day of autumn, according to the old, lunar calendar—and listening to the cicadas in my little garden.

If someone were right now to ask me to list words that have special appeal for me, I would include—and not simply because I have been compelled to spend the summer in the city—*days aflame*. Oddly enough, my fondness for the blazing sun, which developed after I became sixty, has grown stronger year by year. Though at my age I am no longer capable of the energetic way of life symbolized by the passionate sun, I seem to want to live as if I were. And it is better to want to do that and be incapable of it than it is to be indifferent on the matter.

Even in my youth, I did not live passionately. The path I have followed has been ordinary and flat. Now it is covered with a tangle of weeds. This may explain my infatuation with the words *days aflame*. One of my poems, "Evening," explains my feeling.

> *Long rain gone, I*
> *Sit for half a day*
> *In my veranda rattan chair and*
> *Face the garden*
> *Weed-sunk like the years and months of*
> *My past.*
> *Turning back to seek*
> *Days of Triumph*

Days of Disappointment,
All along the long
Straight, weed-choked road,
I cannot tell one from the other.
All I recall:
Days when I dashed toward the
Passionate sunset sky.
When? I do not know.
But frantic and aflame
I strode toward the heavens,
Burning fiery red.
Bathed in the fire powder
Burning the sky, I
And the graveyard of weeds around me
Flamed red too.

As it says in the poem, I do not remember when this kind of thing occurred. But the only times I vividly recall are those when I was striving passionately and desperately to accomplish something. Then I was not merely walking under the hot sun. Instead, I strode into a sky red with the flaming evening sunset. When one is my age, the only things that remain bright and distinct in the memory are times when one has burned to accomplish something, those past times that prove one has lived. All the triumphs and all the disappointments disappear; only the moments of bright, sincere effort—no matter how short they were—retain their luster.

Recently I published a poem called "Summer," part of which I should like to quote for you.

Of all the four,
The season I prefer is
Summer, and the
Time of summer:
The noon, silent with
Languor and death of wind,
The dead-of-night of the day.
Sitting in the rattan chair
Upon my study porch, I look

43

Afar, pursuing
Distant landscapes.
Beyond cyclone posts at the
Distant desert edge,
A silent troupe of camels
Cuts across.
And the passion of voyaging
Only in the languor and death of wind
In the dead-of-night of the day
Brings me calm
Brings me life.

Forgive me for starting out with these exhibitions of my own feelings. Perhaps it is the workings of the dead-of-night of the day in midsummer that has inspired me to write this way.

I am certain that, unlike me, you are right now walking boldly and passionately through days ablaze, and I envy you. I was very moved by the part of your recent letter in which you described your meeting with Jōsei Toda and the decisive effect it had on your life. Not often are human beings granted the opportunity to encounter a person of such scope as Mr. Toda was, to find a person whose ideas coincide with one's own, to show devotion to such a person, thus to plot one's life path, and then always to love and respect that person. In something you wrote earlier, you commented that, if you had not met Mr. Toda, you would not be the person you are. The kind of relation that existed between you two, the ideal one for teacher and disciple, proves that both of you are extraordinary in your own individual ways. Even more important was the intersection of your paths. This is no common occurrence. Obviously you prized and nurtured the relation between you. Still more impressive to me, however, is the fate that brought you together. Jōsei Toda's life was filled with great passion, as is your own. In your poem "Themes," you have said that human lives have characteristic motifs. Your initial meeting with Jōsei Toda set the theme of your life, while you were still young.

When, in early August, I went to my hometown—now called Amagi Yugashima, it is located on the northern slope of Mount Amagi, about halfway down the Izu Peninsula—to pay a visit to the family graves,

I found the village has changed little since my primary-school days there. Though the old-fashioned, clay-walled storehouse where I lived with my grandmother has been pulled down, the family house still looks much as it used to. And, for the short while I was there, I enjoyed the distinctive peace of going to bed at night and waking up in the morning in the old home place.

Though there are many words in Japanese to designate the town or village where one was born and raised and though I have favored different ones at different stages in my life, on this recent visit, I realized that now I prefer to refer to it as the land of my father and mother.

My father died seventeen years ago, my mother, last year. For me, our hometown is, above all, the place where they sleep. Recently, on the second floor of the slightly tilting home of my mother and father, I read one of your collections of poems, *Seinen no Fu* (Song of Youth), and was especially moved by the verse called "Mother," in which you praise the limitless depth, strength, breadth and beauty of mother's love and comment on how good a thing it would be if that spotless, expansive affection could become the foundation of all social relations.

While I was at home, a year after losing my own mother, the by no means original idea of the blessedness of motherhood came to mind, and I recalled a scene in a book by Minoru Toyota in which a father tells his children that, with the passing of their mother, the sole person who considered their sorrows her sorrows and their joys her joys had vanished from the earth.

Seeing that, in your poems, you praise mother love as wider, deeper and stronger than the sea, I recalled an unforgettable verse from a collection called *Kyōshū* (Nostalgia), by Tatsuji Miyoshi.

> *O sea, in our language you contain mother;*
> *O mother, in the language of the French, you contain sea.*

The allusion is to the Chinese character for sea, which includes an element that is the character for mother, and to the French word *mère* (mother), which includes the word *mer* (sea).

I have never written a poem on this subject, but if I ever do, I suspect it will pertain to the sea and not solely to my own mother but motherhood everywhere.

Not long ago, I received a photography album entitled *What Is Mankind? Is There a Tomorrow?* containing work by one hundred and seventy photographers from eighty-six countries and illustrating an exhibition already held in other countries and soon to be held in Japan. I was asked to give my opinions of the book. After examining the shocking proximity of happiness and misery, civilization and barbarity, peace and war existing side by side all over the world, I realized that the possibility of a tomorrow is an issue of incomparable magnitude and severity. Unless the cruel dualities of the world are faced honestly and directly, the creation of a better living place for man will remain dubious.

As might be expected, there are many photographs of mothers in the collection. There are many of perfectly ordinary people, doing perfectly ordinary things. But the isolation of photography gives them new vividness and the power to impress and made me more strongly aware of the unity of all humanity in such fundamental issues as parent-child relations. I am sure I am not alone in believing that it is the mothers of the world who are best qualified to speak out against the conditions prevailing in many lands today. Because of the nature of their role, they can help us cut the complicated knots of modern life, return to fundamental truths and start afresh.

In some of the other poems in your collection, you mention the truth that human lives, like novels and other works of art, have major themes and that human life is the labor of drawing a self-portrait on the white paper of the moment and the future. I agree. There are themes in human lives, and the working out of those themes is our reason for being here. In other words, human life may be no more than the chance to paint one's own portrait on the blank page of the future. My portrait is not yet finished. I am still at work on it. And it is the very incompleteness that gives me courage.

Yasushi Inoue

Abroad and at Home

August 19, 1975

Since returning from Hawaii at the end of last month, I have been staying on the campus of Soka University. Here in Hachioji, the singing of the cicadas is heard less often now and we gradually get the feeling of fall. The evenings are much quieter and cooler here than in the city.

Each of the points you made in your last letter has sunk deep into my mind. Rereading it tonight, in preparation to writing an answer, I experienced a tranquility and exaltation of inexpressible value.

I heard an echo of something awe-inspiring when I read your words, "All the triumphs and all the disappointments disappear; only the moments of bright, sincere effort—no matter how short they were—retain their luster." It may be that I am now approaching the age when I can realize perhaps a part of the truth in those words. There is a gravity and a significance in what you say and in the poems you quote that I am now beginning to understand. I too hope to live my life walking always into the blazing light.

As I said, I have just returned from Hawaii, where you yourself spent two months a number of years ago. I was invited there to attend a conference of members of the Nichiren Shoshu of America (NSA), a group who share my religious beliefs. At night on the day of our arrival, we were treated to a clear southern sky with a brilliant array of stars, a full moon and the sounds of waves rolling in from the reefs as they have done since time immemorial.

The conference was part of "pre-celebrations" for the bicentennial of the founding of the United States, to take place next year. It made me very happy to see the way the members of NSA take a lively part in the life of all the local communities where they find themselves.

The main scene of the conference activities was an artificial island stage about seventy meters in the offing of Waikiki Beach. The Americans, who are fond of wit and jokes, have a number of explanations for this island. Some claim it is a fallen unidentified flying object. Others insist it is a chunk of the fabled Atlantis.

Apart from this artificial island stage, the Hawaiian Islands themselves also attract me in many ways. Perhaps the most interesting thing about the islands is the way they function as a melting pot for many people from many lands. The famous word *Aloha*, used in happy greetings and sad partings alike, represents the spirit of harmony, good will and friendliness essential in so cosmopolitan a place.

There are a large number of Americans of Japanese descent in Hawaii. The present governor of the state, George Ariyoshi, is the first person of his background to occupy this position. I met him for the first time on a stopover in Honolulu on my way home in January of this year and had several opportunities to talk with him on a friendly basis during the recent conference. I understand that his mother and father suffered intense poverty for a long while after moving to Hawaii from Japan. But the family survived and grew until today it is making great contributions to local society. I am sure that people of this kind, not only in Hawaii but also in Los Angeles, San Francisco, Peru and Brazil, will help do away with the old criticism of the Japanese as close and clannish, even when living in other nations, and help generate the impression of Japanese as citizens of the world.

Hawaii is rich in memories for me, since it was the first foreign place I ever visited. This took place shortly after I became president of Soka Gakkai, following the death of Jōsei Toda. In 1960, when a small but growing number of our members—believing that Buddhism, which is a religion with universal appeal and significance, should be taken to people everywhere—were making great achievements abroad, I decided to make the trip. I did so for two reasons. First, the overseas members requested me to come. Second, aware of the imminent need for global vision, I agreed with the old adage to the effect that, if you want to know the world, you must go out into the world.

Travel was not easy in those days. We had no foreign-travel booking offices, and taking foreign currency out of the country was strictly controlled. Furthermore, the flight to Honolulu was nothing like the comfortable eight hours by jet it is today. The present general director of NSA, Mr. George M. Williams, was supposed to meet me at the airport. But when I arrived, he was nowhere to be found. I searched as much as I could, but with no luck. Finally, as it grew late, I gave thought to accommodations for the night and found a room in a partly demolished hotel. On the following morning, enjoying Waikiki in the refreshing early sunlight, I met Mr. Williams and a group of members. It turned out that our failure to convert the time of arrival in our telegram from local Japan time to Hawaiian time had caused the mixup. No harm was done, and we all had a good laugh. But it seems inconceivable now that this was the first step on my long series of world travels.

Forgive my not mentioning it earlier, but together with your letter, I received a copy of the album *What is Mankind?* and was deeply moved by it, as you were. I have little to add to what you have said on the subject except to say that my own conviction is not only that there will be a tomorrow but also that we must create it. Belief in tomorrow and the future is more than optimistic fictionalizing; no matter how difficult the task, we must ensure that tomorrow comes.

I am proud you mentioned my poems in connection with your conviction that mothers are the most qualified people to object to the miserable state of the world today. I am entirely in agreement with you. Mothers can be the source of faith in the future and in mankind that we must have. And I was encouraged at a recent meeting of the Women's Division of our organization when I saw the zeal and vigor of youth that mothers of middle age and more are able to manifest. Women of this kind encourage me to believe mothers can indeed take the forefront in the drive for worldwide peace.

You say that you have written no poems about your mother, and if you ever do, it would be about motherhood in general. Nevertheless, from the references you make to your home village in Izu as the resting place of your parents, I get the impression your mother must have been one of your most important inspirations. A young acquaintance of mine and an ardent fan of yours—he has read everything you have written—got married last year and chose your home village as the place in which to spend his honeymoon. Since he reveres you greatly, he was thrilled to visit your house, play on the bank of the river nearby and gaze at the beautiful local scenery. He believes your work to represent poetry and a nostalgia for the lofty and eternal. He says it is replete with dignity and unified in calm lucidity. It is overflowing with gentleness and the joy of life. It gives the reader courage through its nobility.

Kunio Tsuji says that the elegance, tranquility and lyricism of your writing are especially conspicuous in this age of Japanese literary wastelands. If I may be permitted to add a word, I should like to express my own belief that the idea of motherly love has been the mediator in your thoughts and has inspired you to assume the passionate stance you take toward life.

I do not share your feelings for hometown. You see, my family— they have been dealers in edible seaweed since the time when Tokyo was still known as Edo—have always lived in Tokyo. Perhaps the lack of a hometown feeling is the result of the bigness of the city. Or perhaps it comes from my always having been in my hometown.

A few years ago, when I visited the beautiful Loire Valley in France and saw the old chateaux in their pastoral settings, the greenery, the flowers, the clear streams and the starry night skies, I experienced my first nostalgia for an old home place. After sharing a discussion with some young Frenchmen, the photographer in our party and I returned to the hotel. On the way, I learned that he is from Kamata, in Tokyo, the same part of the city I am from. Then, thousands of miles from home, we both began talking about our city and indifferent to the late hour and the inconvenience of the place—the landing of the hotel staircase—took out pens and paper and began drawing maps of Kamata, showing the sea, the roads, the ponds and the railway lines. We talked about what things used to be like and how they have changed. We compared and corrected each other's memories until my wife laughingly called our attention to the clock. Far away from our hometown, we felt closer to it than we usually do when we are actually in it.

Daisaku Ikeda

Living to the Fullest

A few days ago, while I was chatting with some young people, the subject of life and death and the Buddhist approach to them arose. One member of the group expressed the following opinion: "When I was younger—before I was twenty—I often thought of death and the fear and insecurity associated with it. But I was mainly engaged in dealing with the idea of dying. As I got older, I lost interest in the abstract idea and found myself coming closer and closer to the actual reality. The time I have left to live is shorter than the time I have already lived. But, instead of the fear and anxiety I experienced when I regarded death in the abstract philosophical sense, I am now filled with courage and hope to live what I have left in the best and fullest possible way."

The group tended to disregard what this man said since, though the oldest among them, he was only in his late thirties. Still I could tell he was being sincere.

I am starting this letter in a very serious vein, because I want to explain some of the feelings I experienced from a recent reading of a number of your works, especially the novel *Kaseki* (Fossils), in which you come directly to grips with the issue of death and, consequently, with the issue of life. In the person of the businessman Tajihei Ikki, you set before the reader the real agony and shock of a man facing his own apparently imminent death. The paucity of Japanese novels attempting the same thing indicates the difficulty of the task.

Having arrived in Paris, Ikki suddenly learns that he is ill with an inoperable duodenal ulcer and has only a year to live. He tells no one but is thereafter compelled to engage in a constant inner dialogue with his faithful companion, death. (Though the small print of the edition I read meant I could not do without my glasses, I was impatient when I had to remove them to rest my eyes.) In the following passage, we see how the idea of death has become rooted in Ikki's brain.

"Ikki was never free of the idea of death for even a moment. Death walked with him. In the past, he had spent most of his time with Funazu, his secretary; now he spent all of his time together with death. Its tread echoed his own. When he stopped, it stopped too. It turned the corner when he did.

"He walked in the company of death. At the time yesterday when he had received the phone call from Doctor Shirosaki, suddenly this undesirable fellow traveler had appeared at his side, to remain there. From then on, they had not parted for an instant."

Looking from his hotel window at an elderly person in the nearby park, he says to himself, "This old, lonely person has only a little time left but is determined to live it out. He doesn't know how much time he has, but he wants to make the best of it. I must do the same."

In the extremity of mental agony, Ikki accepts and becomes accustomed to his fatal follower. Then, miraculously, the operation that was

thought impossible is performed, successfully, and death recedes to a distant horizon. The month Ikki lived with death always before his eyes seems a mere fossil of an ancient past. The description of this development is especially stirring. "Everything was fossilized. Madame Marcellin and the whole, slow current of time swirling around her. Everything, fossils. Ikki told himself, 'You can never go into that strange, ringingly taut, dark, transparent time again. You are disqualified. The lofty cherry trees, the Seine, the Roman temple, Madame Marcellin—all fossils now.'"

Then, while trying to resolve the problem of how to live to the maximum from that time forward, he recalls words said to him by a friend on his deathbed. "I want to live so that everything around me remains clean. I want to think about other people more. Pushing people out of the way and trying to climb over their heads are no good. Chasing nothing but money—that's no good either, like knocking your brains out trying to be a little more famous, a little more powerful. To hear the birds' song and to say, 'Ah, they're singing!' To see the flowers and to say, 'Ah, they're blooming!' That's the way to live."

These are only a few parts of the book that I found deeply affecting. I do not intend to attempt to analyze the novel as a work of art; I am not qualified to do that. Nor do I speculate on its meaning. But I do wonder what the key is, what it was that enabled you to come to grips with the philosophical elements of death and to crystallize the results of your thought in a moving, convincing novel. As a work of art, the book stands on its own. Still, if I may ask the question, I would like to know whether it was your own personal experience that prompted you to write it. I feel certain it was something more than the wish of an outstanding literary artist to deal with death as a motif.

My first impression of the book was one of all-pervading light and lucidity. You have managed to treat death without being morbid. From his anxiety and desperation, the hero learns the meaning of living. Your art creates a world hovering between brightness and dimness. Through darkness, you have illuminated darkness. This must be the outcome of your own interpretation of life and death.

I have had weak lungs from childhood and, as a consequence, have often been on the verge of death. Jōsei Toda worried about me and occasionally said he wished he could take years from his own life to lengthen mine, which he feared would be brief. I shall never forget this. And, in all of the times when death has seemed close, I have always resolved to go on, for his sake and for the sake of my mission. I have never been afraid of death. I have never been engrossed in its contemplation, not even when it was apparently very close.

For everyone, life and death are the maximum mysteries. Philosophers and men of religion must discuss them. Heidegger has said that human beings are entities oriented toward death. Buddhism, like all other religions, has a system of thought devoted to explaining this riddle. It is exemplified in the famous tale of the Four Excursions through the City Gates.

While still a prince in his father's house, Shakyamuni made four excursions, one on each of four days, each from a different city gate. When he went out the gate on the east, he encountered an old man; when he went out the gate on the south, he saw a sick man; when he went out the gate on the west, he saw a dead man; and when he went out the gate on the north, he saw an ascetic monk who had abandoned the secular world to search for religious truth. This experience taught Shakyamuni that human life is entirely dependent on the Four Sufferings of aging, illness, death, and birth, which is the cause of the other three. This enlightenment led him to believe that only the search for religious truth could bring relief from these elemental sufferings. Nichiren Daishonin, in writing about death, said that men should first learn how to face their final hour and then address themselves to learning other things.

The meaning of life and how to live it are themes belonging to more than philosophical speculators. In their own, perhaps modest ways, all human beings grope for ways to live better. But all such attempts inevitably entail facing the truth of death. Though it may be only my personal interpretation, I believe your novel *Fossils* teaches that a person can learn to live only after facing the knowledge that, sooner or later, he must die.

No other problem so completely transcends man's reasoning powers as does the issue of life and death. As you have said, we must put our rational abilities to full use wherever they are effectual. However, there are many unexplored regions that cannot be measured on the scale of human reason. In these areas we must call on the assistance of faith.

Man is the only creature on earth aware of self. Since he has the ability to orient himself in terms of past and future, he is fated to be aware of death. It may be inappropriate to use the word *fear* in connection with them, but other animals certainly instinctively demonstrate the will to survive and go on living by resisting death.

In his book *Kinosaki nite* (At Kinosaki), Naoya Shiga describes the thoughts he entertains as he observes a rat about to drown.

"It seemed strange that, obviously doomed, the rat should so desperately try to escape, to save itself. It was unpleasant to watch, it made me sad. . . . No matter how we may long for peace after death, the agitation of the process of approaching death is fearsome. Animals ignorant of suicide must keep struggling until they finally die. What would I do if I were in the rat's place? Probably just what it is doing."

Though each of us should do so, it is hard for people today to break away from the confining concerns of every day and the ordinary flow of time to face the fact of death, because they are too often interested only in the desires and pleasures of the fleeting moment, in the things they can actually see and feel. But we cannot alter the cause-and-effect nature of life. And I believe that your novel *Fossils* is widely loved, especially among the young, because it provides an opportunity to come face to face with the issue of life and death, an issue that modern man attempts unsuccessfully to transcend.

You have said that, as the strength of life ebbs, the human being grows unable to think of anything but his individual self. This is true. Abundant vital living strength cracks the shell of egoism, but its debility brings human beings so low that ultimately they do not think even of their own precious selves. But rich life force—the only cure for the desiccation and selfishness that blight much of modern life—is impossible without the full realization that life and death are two inseparable aspects of one entity.

Daisaku Ikeda

Final Preparedness

September 23, 1975

Thank you for your letter, for having read my book *Fossils*, which I wrote about ten years ago, and for sharing with me your opinions of its basic theme. Perhaps, since I do not yet have any really sound ideas on the subject of life and death, I was out of bounds in writing such a novel. When it appeared in book form, having first been serialized in a newspaper, it was reviewed by a few people. But you are the first person to deal fully with its main topic and its relation to me.

I have been in my Karuizawa workplace since the second half of August. I came here to work out a general plan for a novel on the life of the great tea master Sen no Rikyū [1521–91]. Unfortunately, nothing has come of my efforts.

The most arresting part of his story is certainly the mental state he was in in the brief period between the time Toyotomi Hideyoshi, the military ruler of the nation, ordered him to commit suicide and the time he actually killed himself. But this is a very difficult time to write about. It is entirely likely that Rikyū's truest characteristics would manifest themselves in this last period, but the writer who wishes to describe them has no evidence to go on but the few things Rikyū said and wrote at the time. His parting words to the world took the form of a short poem: "*Seventy years of life; | I scorn the powers around me. | This my precious sword | kills patriarchs and Buddhas alike.*" And there is another short poem in which he says, "*All I have with me, | this one sword, | I now resign to heaven.*" His Zen master Kokei, when he asked Rikyū about his mental state in his last days, was told that it was like fearsome thunder in the midst of a clear day of contentment.

This is vivid literary evidence, but I am afraid that if I tried to use it as material for a novel I would be going astray. I do not believe it is an accurate reflection of the way this revolutionizer and creative innovator would prepare to meet his final hours. It is both difficult and fearsome for me to write precisely about Rikyū's feelings toward his own imminent death.

Shūsui Kōtoku [1871–1911], who was imprisoned and sentenced to death for anarchical acts in the early part of this century, wrote a brief work entitled *Shishō* (Death and life), in which he sets forth his own resignation in the face of death as earnestly and patiently as if he were intent solely on imparting his feelings carefully so that the reader can understand. From the deliberateness of his text, it is possible to obtain an accurate impression of his attitude. The literary evidence in the case of Sen no Rikyū, on the other hand, is in poetry. It is difficult to be certain that one is interpreting absolutely correctly. I do not mean that the poetry is of inferior quality or is invalid as evidence. I believe that when he sat in the room where he was to commit ritual suicide, Rikyū was in a frame of mind other than the one intimated by the poems and had already attained a high degree of resignation that the poems do not reflect.

Recently I have become convinced that direct confrontation with death evokes common responses in all people. The human being takes a good look at life for the first time when he is compelled to take a good look at death. No matter whether the person is religious or not, at this time, the meaning of life, in even its simplest forms, becomes a matter of the greatest urgency.

Seven or eight years ago, at the request of a publishing company, Yoshimi Usui and I jointly edited a collection of essays and philosophical writings in ten volumes, one of which, devoted to the topic of life and death, included twelve or thirteen articles by such people as Taisetsu Suzuki, Kanzō Uchimura, Shinzō Koizumi, Shūsui Kōtoku and yourself. Aside from Christian, Buddhist and other religious writings in which doctrines are based on such considerations, the number of books dealing directly with death and preparedness for it are relatively rare. Death usually comes suddenly, without forewarning, and ordinary people do not think about it until it is close at hand. When the time comes, very few people are cool enough to give concise, written

form to their emotions and impressions. I was pleased with the chance to work on the collection of essays I mentioned because it compelled me to read several outstanding texts on life and death.

As you suspected, for about a year prior to writing *Fossils*, which appeared serially in the *Asahi Shimbun* from November, 1965, until December of the following year, I thought I might have cancer. I grew strikingly thin and was constantly rundown, as members of my family and acquaintances pointed out to me. A friend I had not seen for some time called to invite me to a party to celebrate our long-delayed reunion. When he saw me, he did not recognize me: I had changed that drastically. He told me that he suspected serious illness and urged me to see a doctor without delay. Of course, I underwent a thorough examination at a cancer center, and was told that nothing had turned up. Still I continued to lose weight, had no appetite and was weary most of the time.

About half a year before beginning *Fossils*, with the nagging idea that I ought to see the places I wanted to see while I was still physically able, I traveled to Western Turkistan, Uzbekistan, Tadzhik and Turkmenistan. I saw shock on the faces of the members of my family who came to Tokyo International Airport to meet me at the end of my month-and-a-half journey in the desert. On the following day, they took me to the cancer center, where again tests failed to show anything suspicious. Some physical irregularities were called to my attention, but none of them was likely to be the cause of my debility.

For about the next six months, I suffered from the fear that cancerous cells lurked somewhere that doctors had overlooked. While working or talking with friends, I would suddenly glimpse the great sea of death. Throughout this period, I tried to convince myself that, if I had cancer, there was nothing to be done except calmly come face to face with death in my own way. When the time arrived for me to carry out a promise for a serialized novel, I was coming to the end of what could be called my phase of cancer neurosis. Almost without hesitation, I selected as the motif of the book the theme that you have seen worked out in the novel itself. I felt that if I simply expressed my encounters with death as a companion, it would produce a work of literary merit.

Needless to say, if I had actually been afflicted with cancer and had undergone surgery for its cure, my own dialogue with death-companion would have been different from the ones in the book. The character Ikki resolves to battle with a death that is closing in on him fast, but he is actually expressing feelings I experienced when I suspected the possibility of my own imminent demise. Had I really been stricken with cancer when I undertook to write the story, I seriously doubt I would have made the kind of declaration against death that I have Ikki make.

I am not suggesting that the attitude of the hero of *Fossils* is unreal. There are people who defy death the way Ikki does, and perhaps I would too in a similar situation. But, now, ten years later, I believe that, though the novel is valid because Ikki is finally saved from immediate death, if such had not been the case, he would have been compelled to fight a losing battle with doom.

If I were to write the book now, I would have respect for Ikki's mental state and take a more direct look at his fate. Perhaps it is odd for an author to project the lives of his characters beyond the end of the novel. Still, I suspect that after the conclusion of *Fossils*, Ikki took a more direct, simpler approach to death. I know that I, the creator of the book, would, and Ikki, my creation, probably would too.

Once he had death for a companion, Ikki began to live in a "strange, ringingly taut, dark, transparent time." This seems the appropriate expression to use to describe the time flowing around a person threatened by death. Some other phrase might come closer to accuracy, but explaining the structure of that special kind of time spent in death's company is very difficult. The structure of time changes as the dialogue with death deepens. The time Shūsui Kōtoku spent awaiting death in prison was probably quiet, soft and, at the same time, traversed by something sharp and severe, like a sword.

The important experience of suspecting myself ill with cancer caused me to think of death, and consequently of life. About five years later, I wrote another novel on the same theme—*Hoshi to matsuri* (Stars and festivals)—which would never have come into being except for the earlier *Fossils*.

Now, threatened by cancer or not, I have reached the age where I frequently gaze on death's sea, which is sometimes far, sometimes near. I saw my expanse of death for the first time seventeen years ago, when I lost my father. It was still in the distance then. My father had been a shield between me and death, a shield that prevented my even thinking of it. When he was gone, I suddenly said to myself, "Your turn is next." I had my initial glimpse of the sea of death.

I came closer to its waters when I was afraid I had cancer. Now the sea is a constant part of the landscape, quiet and not all that far away.

A respected fellow writer once said to me, "Well, it's about time you started getting prepared to die." It has been about time for some time now. Prepared to die! I do not know whether I am capable of being that. But I want to try to be.

Yasushi Inoue

Maples, Mountains,
Enchanted Realms

October 18, 1975

When, in early October, I made a trip to Mount Hodaka, the mountainsides were extremely beautiful with red-orange and red-gold maples and the creeping pine below them. Mount Hodaka richly deserves its fame for autumnal foliage. I first made the climb when I was working on a novel called *Hyōheki* (Ice wall) set in this locale. This was my seventh or eighth trip, although the first during the season of the maples. I have never seen it in the depth of winter, when I am sure that it is much more severe than the mountain I have come to know. Since I am not a real mountain climber, I am never likely to see that aspect of its personality. For a man of my age, the seven hours the journey takes and the three hours of steep climbing are exhausting. But the weariness and the hardship vanish under the spell of the red and gold leaves, which continued to surround me mentally in my first waking moments for three mornings after my return to Tokyo.

Last year, when I visited the mountain, it was a little early for the maples, but I was gratified to be able to fulfill the long-cherished wish to descend to Okumatajiro—in spite of the many fallen trees obstructing the path—to pay my respects at the grave of Gorō Wakayama, the model for one of the leading characters in my novel *Ice wall*. The precipices and slopes of Okumatajiro are a fitting setting for the grave of this young mountain climber, whose memorial bears only his name.

I shall probably continue next year to climb the mountain, as I have in the past few years, though I have made a slight alteration in the process. Once I climbed to one of the peaks of the mountain after reaching the lodge at Karasawa. But last year and this year too, deciding the extra exertion was too much for me, I spent the night at the lodge and then went down again. In another five years, I may be unable to climb even that far and will have to be content strolling among the trees on the banks of the beautiful Azusa River.

People ask me why I climb mountains at my age. I always reply that the mountains summon me. This year too I shall hear Hodaka asking me why I do not come and shall forget all my troubles and set out. I am not infatuated or bewitched by the mountain; I first climbed it at the age of fifty when I was already too old for infatuation or enchantment. Moreover, I know nothing about the joys of real mountain climbing. All I know is that, at the beginning of summer or fall, I hear the mountains calling and get the urge to go. I felt the same kind of summons last year when I climbed to four thousand feet above sea level in the Himalayas, which said to me, "Come on, we are big; there is a place even for a non-mountain climber like you."

The classic expression of the relation between the climber and the mountain is this: we climb mountains because mountains are there. This may be a glib way to explain why some men persist in risking their lives to climb higher and higher peaks where no one has ever trod. But I do not especially like the idea. When I first heard the statement, I experienced a vague sense of resistance to it. My reaction is no longer vague. I am disturbed by the arrogance of climbing mountains "because they are there." I dislike the word *conquest* newspaper writers employ to describe the achievements of people who scale new mountain heights. Though it is perhaps no more than a writer's trick, I nonetheless think it wrong to speak of man's conquering any part of the world of nature, before which he should always be humble. Climbers probably understand the grandeur of nature and the vastness of mountains better than anyone else, but if they feel it proper to explain their activities on the sole basis of the mountains' existence, they are mistaken. I have been moved to write to you this way about mountains because of the deep interest I felt in the parts of your dialogue with Arnold J. Toynbee (*The Toynbee-Ikeda Dialogue: Man Himself Must Choose*) in which you mention optimum relations between man and nature.

Yesterday morning the telephone rang. It was a certain magazine asking me to tell them the two or three things that impressed me most this year. Feeling they were jumping the gun or forcing the season, I said, "The maples of Mount Hodaka," and hung up. As soon as I had done so, I realized the editorial staff was not being hasty after all. The next issue of their magazine would be the December one, the last of the year. Suddenly I realized in amazement that the year was nearly gone. What could be the most impressive things in the year, if I thought about the matter seriously?

I had been correct to mention the maples at Hodaka, but perhaps the biggest event for me this year was the trip I made to Kyoto in January to examine seventy paintings by Tomioka Tessai [1836–1924]. Until only a few years ago, I had little interest in this artist, who turned out ten thousand works, including a large number that are attributed to him but that are in fact forgeries. Though he was said to be great, I felt no compatibility with his work, which was certainly extravagant and lively, but which failed to capture me. There was simply no connection between Tessai and me.

But I was interested in the paintings he produced in the traditional genre referred to as pictures of ideal, or enchanted realms. I very much wanted to examine as many of these pictures as possible—especially those from his late years—at one time. I hoped to be able to find out whether Tessai actually longed for the kinds of realms he painted, whether he actually would like to read, think and work in them. I wanted to get into his mind through his pictures. Though enchanted realms are alien to me, I was interested in making an evaluation, not of the pictures themselves but of the imaginary worlds Tessai presents in them.

When a publishing firm asked me to write one volume in a twenty-volume series on famous Japanese paintings, for the sake of my own education, I selected the volume on the works of Tomioka Tessai. To do research for my article, I visited museums and other places in Kyoto, where I saw seventy of his paintings, most of which dealt with ideal, enchanted realms. Of the total, twenty-one were painted when the artist was in his eighties, and most of these late works dealt with enchanted realms. I was delighted.

Going from picture to picture, I kept mentally questioning Tessai: "Would you really like to live in a place like this?" And he kept replying, "Well, if you don't like that one, how about this? Or this?"

From my hasty examination I learned that, without exception,

Tessai's pictures in this genre before his eighty-fifth year represented Chinese-inspired or otherworldly blessed realms. After about the middle of his eighth decade, however, though the compositions were the same, the enchanted lands he painted were bathed in a Japanese sunlight. A Japanese wind blows through them. They have become ideal from the Japanese viewpoint. This trend continues until the calm, bright masterpieces of his eighty-ninth and last year. Even I would like to dwell in the enchanted lands he painted in this phase.

I came to agree with the general evaluation that Tessai got better as he got older and must admit that the masterpieces of his last years are the work of a fine artist. I was moved and touched to see that, after a long career of painting enchanted realms in foreign modes, at the end he made them look like Japan.

Another arresting trend appears in the paintings of the brief period between his eighty-seventh and eighty-eighth birthdays. In these enchanted realms the usual boulders and towered pavilions appear, but they are unpeopled. Water flowing over the rocks forms rapids and waterfalls. And one can imagine how startling such scenes would be in the moonlight. But these uninhabited enchanted lands are bleak and desolate. I feel convinced that in this short period, Tessai must have experienced a deep emotional trauma. Though it is only my guess, there may be a connection between this trend and the death of his son three years earlier.

Brightness and serenity return in the final year. I cannot suppress a doubt, however, that the enchanted realms portrayed in these last paintings are intended to be in any way ideal. I suspect each of them represents the inner world of the artist's mind. Each of these pictures, categorized according to tradition as representations of blessed realms, shows something of the aspirations, dangers, joys and sorrows of the artist. I should like to have another chance to examine all of Tessai's paintings over again.

The maples on Mount Hodaka and closer acquaintance with the work and mind of this painter were two of the most impressive things not only of this past year but of my whole life as well.

Yasushi Inoue

The Beauty of Age

October 22, 1975

The muted grays and whites of the mists frequent here in Kirishima, where I have been staying at our organization's study center for the past week, create romantic autumnal moods, but when they persist too long, melancholy sets in. Fortunately today the weather is fair enough to allow me to look out to Kinkō Bay and to the volcano Sakurajima in the distance. The scale of the scenery inspires spiritual expansiveness. The cool wind tossing the silver-tasseled pampas grass on the mountain slopes and setting the tree branches to whispering is refreshing but oddly sad. Your descriptive powers bring the flaming brilliance of the maples on Mount Hodaka clearly to my mind's eye. The trees here are only beginning to turn, and since I must return to Tokyo in a day or so, I shall probably not see them at their best. Still the first hints of fall color among the leaves have an undeniable charm of their own.

My own congenital poor health and the hectic life I lead have prevented my enjoying mountain climbs like the ones I learn—to my surprise, I must confess—you make. Nonetheless, I am convinced, the wordless call of the mountains is precisely as you describe it.

While strolling in the highlands here, I have examined the book of Tessai's paintings you kindly sent together with your letter. I have in the past been relatively familiar with the ink landscape paintings of such artists as Ike no Taiga [1723–76], Yosa no Buson [1716–83] and Watanabe Kazan [1792–1841], but, to be frank, until now I have had no special interest in Tessai. Reading your essay and examining the pictures, however, have stimulated me to want to do a little study on this painter on my own.

I know practically nothing about Tessai's attitude toward life, but I seem to be able to judge something of his vigor from his pictures and from the way in which they reveal the full gamut—the so-called five colors—of black ink. The pictures of his last period, the years immediately preceding his death, are especially vigorous. And his revelation of power at the close of life has led me to reflect on the beauty of age.

The Kirishima center is a place where members of our organization from Japan and abroad come together to relax and pursue their own courses of research. Not long ago, members from Brazil came to enjoy fellowship with members from Japan. Among the visitors was an elderly woman who had emigrated to Brazil decades ago and who had not seen Japan since then. After many years of toil, sweat and hardship, she now owns a fine farm in the inner Amazon region. She related to me not only her joy at seeing her homeland again, but also the gratitude—almost awe—with which she regards her whole life and all its experiences. I found her extremely beautiful. Each of the wrinkles on her sun-browned face spoke of a hardship or some suffering she has survived and profited by. Like all other maxims, the old saying that hardship gives life its luster is only half true: it is not experiencing suffering but surviving and conquering it that makes human life brilliant. Only people who have won the battle with the tempests and storms of the world verify the maxim. I see the value of Tessai's whole life in the masterpieces of his eighty-ninth year, and I think the face of this unknown old woman from Brazil rivals Tessai's masterworks in terms of beauty.

In spite of the negative interpretations often put on it, the process of growing old, which none of us can elude, might be thought of as a desirable summation, a culmination of everything in life. The true evaluation of a person's worth comes only at the end. A life that has been tempered and polished through long experience and victory gleams bright at the close. A life spent in laziness and gloom will end in misery.

The beauty of age, the grace of growing old, deserves more respect than beauty at any other stage of life. The glory of the autumnal years is like the maples in their final crimson and gold. The beauty of youth, like that of fresh new verdure, is incomparably dazzling but shallow. It contains the incipient peril—or promise of peril—of its own failing and decay. The beauty of age is a deeper one of promise fulfilled.

Romain Rolland has described the wonderful face of Tolstoi after eighty-two years of constant struggle and genius in the following way:

"His face had taken on definite lines; had become as it will remain in the memory of men: the large countenance, crossed by the arch of a double furrow; the white, bristling eyebrows; the patriarchal beard, recalling that of Moses of Dijon. The aged face was gentler and softer; it bore the traces of illness, of sorrow, of disappointment, and of affectionate kindness. What a change from the almost animal brutality of the same face at twenty, and the heavy rigidity of Sebastopol! But the eyes have always the same profound fixity, the same look of loyalty, which hides nothing and from which nothing is hidden." [*Tolstoy*, Romain Rolland, tr. by Bernard Miall, London and Leipsic, 1911: T. Fisher Unwin]

As is well known, in his last year Tolstoi left home only to fall fatally ill in an obscure village in the cold of winter. At the end, he is supposed to have wept, not for himself but for the unhappy people of the world. According to the report, he said, "Why do you trouble yourselves over me when there are millions of people suffering on earth?" No matter whether these were actually his words, his face in the last phase of his life is a concentration of the spirit these words symbolize.

Although her face is not familiar to the whole world, as Tolstoi's is, the old woman from Brazil has left an indelible impression of love-filled tenderness, depth, sincerity and victory over hardship on my mind.

I began this letter at Kirishima and am now forced to conclude it in Tokyo in very sad circumstances. I have just received word of the death of Arnold J. Toynbee. To my grief, it is now necessary to refer to this great historian in the past tense. He was a great figure in this century, a man who formed a connective link between the cultures of the East and West. It seems only yesterday that I sat talking intimately with him in preparation for the book *The Toynbee-Ikeda Dialogue*, to which you have kindly alluded in our correspondence. In some of your recent work, you speak of the unique nature of each human encounter. For me, the meeting with Arnold J. Toynbee was certainly a once-in-a-lifetime happiness. You have mentioned a fondness for the spirit behind the Japanese expression *ichiza konryū*, meaning a striving on the part of all parties involved to make a complete, significant success of whatever they undertake: drama, tea ceremony, poetry reading and so on. This spirit is needed not only in the performing arts but also in all aspects of life. The human aim ought to be the search for harmony and cooperation of the kind implied in the words *ichiza konryū*. Throughout the long course of his life, Arnold J. Toynbee earnestly participated in just such a search.

Daisaku Ikeda

Surviving and Overcoming

November 17, 1975

I arrived in Hiroshima two or three days before our annual general meeting, held on the ninth of this month, for the longest stay I have ever spent in the city. Our decision to hold the meeting here is related to the thirtieth anniversary of the termination of World War II and to our determination to exert maximum effort to prevent the recurrence of the monstrous tragedy of atomic bombing anywhere in the world. On the day before the meeting, as I made a modest floral tribute and bowed my head in prayer before the Peace Park memorial to the victims of the bombing, many thoughts ran through my mind.

Today little is left in the bustling, thriving city to tell of the inferno it was on that day thirty years ago. The people themselves seem to have forgotten. But as I stood in the gentle autumn sunlight under the evergreen trees, I felt deeply aware of the possibility that the pain of those horrible times is still present, though latent, and that it can be easily evoked again. The atomic bombing has a meaning too deep, too enduring, to be eroded by the mere passage of time. My deepest hope is that through preserving the memory of Hiroshima we can provide the whole world with a guideline for future thought and action. So far, what has been achieved in the right direction is insufficient. In spite of the ponderous lesson of the bombings, nuclear arms are far from outlawed. In fact, their number is on the increase.

I watched the proceedings of the twenty-fifth symposium against nuclear weaponry, held in Kyoto in August of this year, with very close attention and was deeply moved that the famous physicist Hideki Yukawa should consider it essential to disregard his ill health and appear at the conference in a wheelchair to express anxiety over the growing number of nations in the world possessing nuclear arsenals.

On the basis of maximum respect for the inestimable value of human life, our organization has consistently advocated abolition of nuclear weapons and last year conducted a campaign in which a petition with ten million signatures was drawn up for the total elimination not only of nuclear weapons but also of all warfare. As I have mentioned to you before, our peace movement is based on the philosophy of Buddhism and on the thought of my mentor, the late Jōsei Toda, who always insisted that anyone who would use nuclear weapons is a devil taking away or threatening to take away precious life. The demonic spirit, though generally manifest in individuals or groups, is actually inherent in life itself. It is essential to battle with this menace at life's deepest levels, and this is precisely what our organization has set out to do.

Life persists with amazing pertinacity. The book *Matsuri no ba* (Festival place), which you admire and which won the Akutagawa Literary Prize this year, is based on the experiences the author, Kyōko Hayashi, underwent in Hiroshima at the time of the bombing. At one

point, she says, "In November, three months after the atomic bomb fell, plants were budding in the burned ruins. The power of life, inherent in the earth, was already at work again." In *Haikyo-kara* (From the ruins), a short story by Tamiki Hara [1905–51], occurs this passage: "Suddenly I heard a baby's faint cry. My ears were not deceiving me. As I walked, the voice became clearer and clearer. It was strong. It was suffering. It was totally innocent. People could live in such a place! A baby could cry there! And the very idea caused an indescribable emotion to grip me in the bowels." This author shows the way in which life must and will go on, sometimes under the most impossible circumstances.

Accompanying me as I placed flowers at the memorial to the Hiroshima dead were two young people, members of what is called the Hiroshima second generation. Born at about the time of the tragedy, their infant voices may have been among those totally innocent ones Hara describes in his short story. They too illustrate the persistence of life. But they reveal more. Both of them suffered the effects of nuclear radiation. The young man did not face this curse until he was in the second year of junior high school, when he suddenly, inexplicably, fell ill. He grew increasingly sluggish. A tumor on his neck required surgery, which forced him to remain out of school for a year. In desperation, one day his mother broke down, crying that her son's illness was the fault of an apple she had eaten that day when the black atomic rains fell on Hiroshima after the bombing. Thereafter, the boy lived constantly in death's shadow. His mother and then his grandmother died. He himself contemplated suicide.

The other person helping me with the floral tribute was a lively young lady. While in junior high school, perhaps because both of her parents had been exposed to secondary radiation at Hiroshima, she began suffering from severe anemia. Her nose bled incessantly and red splotches disfigured her skin. Later even the slight damage done by an injection needle caused her blood vessels to burst. Purplish marks covered her body.

But both of these young people have survived. More important, they have triumphed to emerge from the pit of despair and suffering and put their grim experiences to use in our movement for world peace. The young lady wrote the following in her contribution to a book of recollections of Hiroshima victims, published last year under the title *Hiroshima no kokoro nijū-ku nen* (The Hiroshima spirit, twenty-nine years):

"We members of the second generation of atomic-bombing victims are doomed to face issues of recurrence [of pathological symptoms] and of hereditary influence. To be frank, I find this terrifying. Still, I have resolved to live out my life with courage. Should someone ask me what I consider the meaning of the peace movement to be, I would reply, 'For me it means surviving, getting married and raising healthy children. In other words, the peace movement means constantly proving that I can live every day, fully, just like all other human beings.' "

Neither of these two young people holds grudges against the past. They do not feel victimized and are not sorry for themselves. Both have a firm understanding of the meaning of their lives. Their clear eyes radiate the strength and will to live for the future. At the general meeting of our organization, I made some comments on the problem of nuclear weapons, and as I did so, those two young people were in my mind's eye.

One of the subjects of the meeting was the issue of health and youth, our organization's major topic for the coming year. Both are of fundamental importance, since, without the breath of good health and youthfulness in every home, peace and happiness for all society will be difficult to attain. By *youthfulness* I do not mean only chronological, physical youth. The spirit of youth is something that has permeated the entire lifetimes of all the leaders who have done great things in world history. In many of these people, it took the form of warmth and concern for others. When Gautama the Buddha lay ill and near death under the Twin Sala Trees, the ascetic Subhuti came to see him. Realizing his master was in very weak condition, Ananda, the Buddha's close attendant and disciple, denied the ascetic access. But out of warmth and compassion, the Buddha told Ananda to allow the venerable old man to draw near and he would gladly answer whatever questions he had to ask. In my opinion, the Buddha's attitude represents the warmth of a young life force, a warmth that lasts until the very brink of death.

I am now approaching my forty-eighth year. On my next birthday, I shall encounter, for the fifth time, the year of the dragon, in which I was born. Of the twelve ancient Chinese zodiacal symbols, the dragon

73

alone is a mythological beast. It is a creature associated with extensive legend and romance. For instance, Longmen (Dragon Gate), in Shanxi Province, China, is located at the place where the Yellow River swirls in violent rapids. Fish are rare there. It is said that any that do manage to swim this far acquire supernatural powers and become dragons.

The hour of the dragon is about eight o'clock in the morning, the time when the sun is rising into the sky in its full, glorious might. Though I put no store in astrological superstitions, I see no harm in celebrating the year of one's birth in connection with the animal traditionally associated with it, as a kind of landmark along the road of life. I hope I can always be as vitally alive as the mythical dragon, or the real morning sun, rising into the sky.

Daisaku Ikeda

The Elderly and the Dragon

November 23, 1975

Ready for winter, in the chill, light rain this morning, most of the trees that are going to shed their leaves have already lost them. The few remaining leaves, yellow and brown, hang wet on the one or two ginkgo, maple and other deciduous trees in my small garden. The azaleas and magnolias in the corner still wear their foliage but will be naked in less than two weeks. I do not know when I began considering the short period of autumnal rains something special. But as I sit now in my study, looking out on my drenched plot of grass, earth and trees, I realize I do think it special. And reading your letter makes me thoughtful about many things, including several difficult social problems.

The most amazing and touching part of the letter is your description of the young man and young woman, second-generation victims of the atomic bombings, who, like plants budding in the ruins, survived to conquer despair and fear and to be spiritually reborn to participate in a movement for world peace.

I am in complete agreement with what you said in your speech about the necessity of good health and youthfulness in the individual and the home if peace and happiness are to be ensured. These ordinary words, *health* and *youth*, signify two of the most beautiful things in human life, as everyone ultimately must realize. I have already reached the age when I know too well that, without the spirit of "lifetime youthfulness" that you speak of, all kinds of work are impossible. This reflection on youth inevitably led me to contemplate the problems of aging.

Too often in recent times, the newspapers tell of elderly people living alone, dying and remaining undiscovered corpses for long periods. All of us are ineluctably fated to grow old. None can escape aging of mind and body. Nonetheless, it would be wonderful if, in the face of inevitable fate, all people could live youthfully and vitally until the end.

On park benches in cities like Paris and New York, one frequently sees lonely old people eating meager meals in solitude. People who have worked all their lives and have raised families should not have to face such loneliness in their last years. Though the remnant of the family system persisting in Japan means that old people eating on park benches are rarely encountered, everywhere in the world, to some extent, the elderly find themselves listless and lonely.

In Sweden, which has the most thorough and effective social security program in the world, elderly people stroll the streets of cities like Stockholm and enjoy eating and drinking in the cafes and restaurants, with no sense of getting in other people's way or of being out of place or unwanted. Still, the sight of them wandering aimlessly around with nothing to do is saddening. In the white nights of the far north, wearing hats and carrying canes, they gather in the stone-paved plaza behind the royal palace. Some are flushed with drink. But they are mournful in the pale illumination of the sky. Saving the elderly from being a burden on their children by guaranteeing them food and board, the government simultaneously frees the children not only of the responsibility but also of the desire to care for their parents in their old age.

In this land of the most advanced social security system, suicides among the old are more numerous than anywhere else. The elderly are assured of security without hardships, but they lack those special happinesses and joys that would give them an important reason for going on. Social security is important in solving the problems of the aged, but the high rate of suicides in Sweden proves it is not the whole answer.

The lifetime youthfulness of which you speak is needed by the old as well as the young. As long as senility does not attack mind and body, the old must try to live youthfully till the end. But the ability to do so is not something acquired overnight. Only those who have been vigorous in the prime of life can expect to be correspondingly vigorous in their declining years. I intend to try to do this.

A few days ago, a friend asked me to write something brief for him. I replied with this passage:

"When the children have made the house quiet by going to the equestrian park to fly kites, my thoughts turn to myself. I no longer go out to the plazas or into the cold-congealed fields to fly a kite. I have no kite to fly. But I have come to want—to feel I must—send something high and kitelike into the sky to dance, to soar and to run wild in the wild winds."

The lines are based on recollections of the first day of this year, which is now nearly over. I hope the feeling expressed will be more than a recollection, will become a note on which to begin the coming year. I sent nothing kitelike into the sky this year. But I still want to and suspect the desire will stay with me next year too. I very much like your idea of "lifetime youthfulness."

Let me take this opportunity to congratulate you and wish you the best of continued health on your forty-eighth birthday and your fifth encounter with the year of the dragon. You are about to enter the stage in life of the strongest, most fruitful work. I have no doubt the second half of your life will be even more fulfilled than the first, which, in spite of the difficulties you have sometimes faced, has been rich. I was most gratified to sense from the tone of your last letter that you intend to make it so.

I share your fondness for the dragon—the symbol of the year of your

birth—especially the image of this mythical creature breathing flame as it soars into the sky. In September of last year, while in China, I had a chance to see the astrolabe at the Zijinshan Observatory in Nanjing. The Chinese first devised astrolabes for the observation of positions of stars two thousand years ago. In the Yuan dynasty [c. 1280–1368], a man named Guo Shoujing revised and improved the device so that two people could use it to observe the same star at the same time. The three bronze loops and their various chains on the Zijinshan observatory astrolabe give the appearance of the skeleton of a reptile. A bronze dragon wraps its body around the supporting framework. The complicated astrolabe strongly attracted me because of the combination of a delicate piece of astronomical equipment and a mythological beast. I saw it in the daytime but could imagine how it would look at night, when the dragon would seem to be exhaling flames against all the glittering stars of the sky. This is only my own lyrical interpretation; still the ancient Chinese astronomers' calling on the aid of the dragon in their searches of the heavens and the manifestation of the need to do so in the design of the astrolabe are endearing and graceful. I suspect that at your side, as you work, there is a fire-breathing dragon of good omen on guard.

You mention a Longmen (Dragon Gate) in your letter. In May of this year I was permitted to visit another Longmen, the famous site of the Buddhist cave temples near Luoyang. The recorded 1,352 caves, 750 niches and 39 stone towers of Longmen were all built between the end of the fifth century and the middle of the eighth (that is, from the time of the transferral of the Wei capital to Luoyang to the Xuanzong era of the Tang dynasty). Today we are permitted to see only a small part of the vast extent of these caves, but even what is open to the public impresses the mind with the profound faith that must have inspired people of the past to create these monuments as offerings in the name of Buddhism. The site they chose for images and cave-mansions is the stone walls of the ravine above the beautiful rushing waters where the dragon is born.

Yasushi Inoue

A Dazzling Peak, Dialogues

December 14, 1975

There were seventy students in my graduating class at Numazu Middle School. At the end of last month, about half of us gathered in the city of Fujinomiya for a class reunion. Many of us had not met since we finished school and had no idea—or not enough of an idea to pretend to any real knowledge—of the paths that the rest had been following, the occupations they had entered and the families they had raised. A war had intervened between the periods of our youth and our middle age. Each of us had experienced both good and bad times, both happiness and sorrow. But at the reunion, all these things we kept to ourselves. All of the talk was of shared memories of childhood, the carefree, happy time, memories that brought laughter, joking and some deep emotion.

We drove to Fujinomiya, taking the route around the base of Mount Fuji. For a long while we enjoyed the sight of the snow-clad mountain through the leafless trees. It was now on our right, now behind us. Finally, when the bright red sun went down behind it, I realized how long it had been since I had been thrilled by the beauty of Japanese winter scenery.

As a child in my home village on the Izu Peninsula, I grew up in the daily presence of a little Mount Fuji far in the distance. In Numazu, I lived with the mountain in the guise it assumes from there. So I have a special feeling of intimacy with Mount Fuji, but I do not recall ever having seen it in its snowy entirety in quite the way I did during this drive. For all of that and the next day, as I enjoyed the company of the dazzling peak both in the evening and at dawn, I came to realize it has a scale and glory of its own, a beauty quite unlike that of the Himalayas.

On the day after the reunion, I visited the Fuji Art Museum, which you founded, in the grounds of the Taiseki-ji temple, where there was a display of works from the Tretyakov and Pushkin galleries in Moscow. An exhibition of works from Zagorsk was, I was told, slated to open the next day. I vaguely recalled having seen some of the works on display when I visited the Pushkin and Tretyakov galleries on a trip to Russia a number of years earlier. But seeing them again made me deeply aware of the inadequacy of a single trip to a museum. Unfortunately, the class reunion schedule did not allow me to spend as long at the Fuji museum as I would have liked, but the brief hour I had was a rich luxury. One of the two Russian ladies who explained the exhibition to us had read my book *Oroshiya koku suimutan* (Tales of intoxication with Russia) in a Russian version and was on friendly terms with Mr. B. Raskin, who did the translation. In a manner different from the efficient one in which she went about the business of guiding us through the gallery, she imparted this information to me as we were getting ready to leave. I was very pleased.

This month I have at last started work on the novel about Sen no Rikyū [1521–91], which I have been planning for a long time and have never been able to get around to. For a while, it will be all Rikyū with me. Although I have looked over the majority of the major studies and historical works on the subject, when I begin to write, there will without doubt still be things to research. My attention as a novelist will be concentrated on two topics: the nature of the subtle, refined changes Rikyū worked in the tea ceremony and the way he died. I am interested in both topics but realize they are troublesome to deal with. Since I should not be discussing the theme and structure of a novel I have just started, I will stop with the remark that, having now announced the initiation of the work in this letter, I will be obliged to carry out this long-postponed task. I cannot turn back now.

Now that it is the middle of December, I think more and more about the close friends who have died. Only last month, Genyoshi Kadokawa, president of the Kadokawa Shoten publishing company, died without giving me a chance to thank him for the complimentary copy of his major work *Katarimono bungei no kenkyū* (Study of the narrative work), which he had sent me. I think I told you in a letter in June about having received word of the death of the writer Shōgo Nomura while I was in Beijing. Now Kadokawa, who like Nomura was close to me, is gone. When my book *Hoshi to matsuri* (Stars and festivals) came out in the Kadokawa paperback library early this year, Kadokawa wrote a commentary for it. His attitude in doing so was not so much that he had been requested, but that he had been privileged, to undertake the task.

Each time a friend dies, for a few days—from the time I receive word until the funeral—I hold a perfectly natural dialogue with the departed. Of course, actually I am only talking with myself, but I always feel as if I am telling that person the things I ought to have said to him during his lifetime.

Two living people can rarely ever speak the full truth to each other. When one partner dies, the other can say all that is on his mind and the deceased can neither object nor defend himself. No true dialogue can take place between them. For several days after I learn of a friend's death, however, I virtually negate it by being unable to believe it has happened. This means that for a brief while I talk to him as if he were still alive and yet am able to tell him all the things I should have told but could not tell him while he was actually alive. Of course, this does not constitute a dialogue. But, in this brief span of time, I can converse with the lost friend in a way different from the way the living speak with the living and different from the way the living speak with the dead. And, after the death of a dear friend, I invariably experience the sorrow of saying at last and for the first time the most important things I have to say. I am then grieved by the sadness of human acts.

Though late in doing it, when Kadokawa died, I thanked him for what he had done for me and told him everything I had long wanted to say. Then I included all of this in the message I read at his funeral.

My period of converse with the dead seems to have something in common with the custom, widespread among ancient Japanese aristocrats, of establishing a time (called *mogari*) in which the recently deceased are believed to inhabit a realm between death and life where contacts with the living are possible. In other words, during *mogari* relations different from those between living and living and different from those between living and dead were believed to be establishable. I have read an article by a specialist in Japanese literature who insists that the elegies in the *Manyōshū* poetry collection (compiled in the eighth century) were not ordinary, formal funeral dirges but poems to be recited during the special *mogari* period. Though all poetry of this kind is distinguished by sorrow and sadness, the *Manyōshū* elegies do indeed give the impression of words of love expressed directly to the departed—if I may be forgiven for once again intruding with my own practices—just as I speak directly with my deceased friends for a short while after their deaths.

I deal with the *mogari* custom in the novel *Hoshi to matsuri*, but in his commentary on it Kadokawa did not mention the subject at all. He neither affirmed nor rejected my opinions. Since he had studied with Shinobu Origuchi [1887–1953] and therefore had specialized knowledge on the subject, he probably would like to have commented. He may have hesitated out of courtesy or pity, since whatever he had to say would have been no more than contact between the living and the living.

Yasushi Inoue

Trust between the Living

December 15, 1975

I am very happy that you visited the Fuji Art Museum. In the middle of last month, I too had a chance to see the works from the Tretyakov and Pushkin galleries on exhibition there. Though I lay no claim to erudition in the field of art, I am deeply grateful my visit to the Soviet Union has resulted in cultural exchange of this kind. As you know, the Tretyakov is the largest museum of purely Russian art in the Soviet Union. The Pushkin Museum houses an extensive collection of non-Russian works. While I was pleased that the Pushkin sent us pictures by such masters as Gauguin and Cezanne, I personally am more interested in the paintings from the Tretyakov, because of the lively and intimate impression they give of the real lives of the Russian people.

Forests and vast expanses of land suggesting equally vast stretches of time and the long history of man living with nature characterize the Russian countryside. These features can still be appreciated only short distances from such modern cities as Moscow and Leningrad. Many of the landscapes in the pictures from the Tretyakov—"Ploughing" by Krot, "Wildflowers at the Forest Edge," "The Northward Way," and so on—reveal simultaneously the Russians' intimate love of nature and their awe in the face of its severity.

Others of the Tretyakov pictures recall for me the warmth and hospitality of the Russian people. This trait is symbolized in my memory by the electrically operated mannequin of a woman holding the traditionally hospitable loaf of bread topped with salt and standing in front of the Moscow restaurant called the Slavyanskiy Bazaar, where such notable figures as Tolstoi, Tchaikovsky, Turgenev and Chaliapin used to eat and where I was once invited to share a meal with members of the staff of the University of Moscow. While there, I learned that the first work ever painted on commission by the great Russian painter Repin (it is called "Slavic Bards") was given to this restaurant.

The painting "Sleeping Children" by Petrov was especially heartwarming. In the innocent faces of the two ragged children sleeping close together in the soft sunlight I see a symbol of the determination, profoundly inherent in human life, to overcome hardship and sorrow. From the several books I have read about Repin, I have learned that, when he began working in Moscow, he observed works by some young Moscow artists and said, "I do not know where to start. My eye lights on something. Everywhere things are vitally alive. The drawings reproduce life as it is. Everything is rich in faithful expressive powers. What wonderful pictures! They are so creatively powerful that the eyes find it difficult to believe." In these works he was able to understand a source inspiring creative activity, and this attitude helps explain the vigor of his own work. Unfortunately, his famous painting "Volga Boatmen" was not available for loan, for it certainly reveals Repin's emotional and spiritual intensity. But I have gone on too long on a subject about which I have interest but no specialized knowledge, when my only intention was to thank you for visiting the exhibition.

It has now started to get cold, and whenever that happens, I always remember Tsunesaburō Makiguchi, the first president of our organization, who died in a cold prison cell during World War II. On the evening of November 17, the night before the day on which he actually passed away, we held memorial services marking the thirty-second anniversary of his death. The following day was the forty-fifth anniversary of the founding of the Sōka Kyōiku Gakkai (Value-creating Educational Society), the forerunner of our present organization.

At the time when he founded the group, President Makiguchi was principal of the Shirogane Elementary School, Meguro, Minato Ward, Tokyo, a school that boasts several famous, nationally honored graduates, for example the literary critic Hideo Kobayashi, the novelist Jirō Osaragi and Hitoshi Kihara. Tsunesaburō Makiguchi played an energetic and enthusiastic part in training people of this kind who were to become literary figures of great merit. The three-story reinforced-concrete building in which the school is located, and where it plans to hold

84

centennial celebrations next year, was erected during Makiguchi's tenure as principal. I am very familiar with it, since I often visited the home of Jōsei Toda, our second president, which was just across the street. Mr. Makiguchi's photograph, which hangs on the wall of the principal's office along with those of the other men who have held that position, possesses the dignity and strength of a man who has devoted himself entirely to the search for a new educational system and the study of ways to enrich and improve human life.

In everything, especially in the production of the book *Kachi-ron*, published while he was still principal, he was extremely severe with himself—as sharp as an autumn frost. In connection with the publication of this book, he wrote, "With no pretentions to either learning or ability, the author of *The Philosophy of Value-creation* has been sorely perplexed these ten years, delving into the profound problem of value. The question of value has grown in my mind like a cancer, since I ran up against a problem hard enough to make me lose not only my front but my back teeth also. Even now, I am struggling for the solution, but because of the urgent situation which allows of no further procrastination, as a last resort, after long and desperate efforts, this work has been brought out."

But to the weak or suffering he was compassion itself. He had the true educator's love of children. Once when he was visiting a friend, the conversation grew so interesting that he stayed unwittingly until suppertime. Curried rice was being served, and his portion was brought into the room for guests, as was proper. But he took up his dish and moved at once into the adjacent room to eat smilingly with a noisy band of children he had heard laughing and playing there. On another occasion, when a woman who had visited him prepared to depart, carrying her infant baby on her back in the traditional Japanese fashion, it began to rain. Mr. Makiguchi followed them part of their way, holding an umbrella over the child. When it became imperative for him to turn homeward, he improvised a canopy of several layers of paper to protect the child from the rain.

Memories of Tsunesaburō Makiguchi and Jōsei Toda, both of whom devoted their lives to the religious revolution, will be a mainstay for me as long as I live.

I am not informed on ancient Japanese customs and have therefore nothing to add to your fascinating discussion of the *mogari* period in which, according to very old ways of thinking, the departed exist in an interim realm between the world of the living and the world of the dead. Still your discussion inspired me to ponder this issue from the standpoint of Buddhist beliefs, in accordance with which human beings are born, live, die and then experience a fourth stage intermediate between death and life. This fourth stage is probably comparable to what you mean by the *mogari*. Traditionally the Buddhist postmortem period is thought to last from a minimum of one to a maximum of seven weeks, during which the future fate of the departed life is determined. For this reason, Buddhists pray earnestly for the future happiness of the deceased over a period of seven weeks following death.

At the heart of this tradition is the fundamental Buddhist belief in transmigration and the eternally repeating cycle of life, death, life, death, and so on. Modern man's blindness to all but the visible, tangible world inspires him to reject this theory on intellectual grounds. But it nonetheless deserves respect as the result of the sincere efforts of Buddhist thinkers to interpret the things in the world that are neither visible nor tangible.

I am quick to find truth in your idea that, during something like the *mogari* period, dialogues of a kind impossible between the living and the living or the living and the long dead can take place between the living and the recently dead. What you have said in this connection is of great importance in the effort to discover optimum human relations. In even the most sincere conversation, obstacles, formalities, dignity and disposition invariably hinder total candor. Furthermore, most of us optimistically imagine that there will always be another chance to meet and carry the discussion forward; consequently, it does not matter if a few things go unsaid. And, as we tolerate them, little by little the unsaid things mount up. Their numbers are greater, the closer the relations between the two parties and the more frequent their chances for conversation. In the final analysis, we all, even the most carefree of us, remain conscious of barriers forcing us to create a mental residue of things we ought to, but cannot, utter. Upon the sudden death of a close friend, all of the countless words and memories, stored up so long that many of them have passed from the realm of conscious awareness, gush forth. The friend's departure is the contributory cause—to use

Buddhist terminology—evoking all of these things from the subconscious and making possible a dialogue with the departed.

Still one other factor contributes to this possibility. No matter how well a person may know another, mystery still surrounds parts of the other person's life. During the friend's lifetime, this mystery makes complete frankness difficult. But once the friend is dead and enclosed in the perfection of the past, the mystery loses significance. The surviving person can now enter directly and with complete freedom into the part of his friend's life that he knew. Sorrowfully, but undeniably, the complications of human life prohibit us from being totally open with each other until something like the time of *mogari*.

In his book *Mujō to iu koto* (Mutability), Hideo Kobayashi says that we interpret incorrectly the usual notion that all memories are pleasant. The pleasant nature of memories does not mean we deliberately decorate the past; the past does not allow us to recall more than we need.

In the long run, the dialogue between the living and the dead amounts to the confession and direct emotional expression of the living, though it can be thought of as a dialogue within the mind of the survivor. The candor of this mental exchange gives a hint about the way we ought to react toward each other while still alive. We ought to feel the need to take the other partners of our dialogues directly into our own lives and attempt to enter directly into theirs. Trust is essential if we are to accomplish this—trust that makes possible the union of the self with the other. Buddhism places primary significance on the kind of trust called faith, because it is the secret to the mutual union of all life. On the basis of trust, true dialogue becomes possible between the living and the living, and such dialogue is the starting point for enriching the lives of both parties.

I am glad that you are now working on the book on Sen no Rikyū, which you mentioned to me once during one of our meetings. You are turning your powers of human observation on a subject pregnant with meaning for all Japanese. I eagerly look forward to seeing the outcome of your observation in literary form. Please let me conclude this letter with best wishes for a Happy New Year.

Daisaku Ikeda

Battle Comrade

I hope you are enjoying the warm sunshine of these first weeks of the New Year. Although the change from one year to another may mean no radical alterations in the state of things, it is always pleasant to make a fresh start, and the New Year does give us all an opportunity to do just this.

I have been in the Kansai district since the eighth of the month. As a much younger man, I spent a great deal of time in Osaka, sometimes struggling hard with my work and sometimes enjoying the city and its distinctive mood.

I note from my diary for the year 1957 that, after the first three days of the New Year holiday, I went directly to Osaka.

> January 4 (Wednesday). Departed on the express train *Tsubame* at nine o'clock in the morning for Osaka.
> January 5 (Thursday). On the night train *Gekko*, I returned sadly to my home. On the train I thought of the eternal, the uncreated. I am disturbed about my mental inadequacies. I am profoundly convinced I have no method to follow, no way, except the strong and sincere faith that brings forth the attainment of Wisdom. Oh, mortals!
> January 6 (Friday). Arrived in Tokyo by night train—past nine thirty. Along the way the train made many unscheduled stops, and I was in my seat for eleven hours. To my tired body the energy of Tokyo Station was beyond all wondering. Society and humanity.
> January 16 (Monday). In Osaka. The light is that of approaching

spring. Hopes well up, calling to my heart to fly upward to the sky, big, like the universe. Refreshing blue sky.

These excerpts from my old diary should suggest how I shed my young sweat in Osaka. I made friends while here, but many of them have already died, some at ripe old ages, others far too young. A group of people met me on the evening of my arrival this time, and talking and sharing memories and recollections of the friends who are no longer with us, we lost track of time. This made our gathering all the warmer. Each of the ones who are gone is dear to all of us, no matter how long or short the time we had together. The value of a human life is measured by its contribution to society, not by its length.

I told you in an earlier letter about visiting the Loire Valley. During that trip, I had a chance to see the house where Leonardo da Vinci spent his late years. Of all the interesting and historically valuable things displayed there, the most impressive to me were some words of Leonardo's engraved on a copper tablet. They express succinctly what I consider an accurate evaluation of the worth of human life.

A full life is long.
Full days bring sound sleep.
A full life gives a tranquil death.

The news I received on the morning of January 9 that Zhou En-lai had died chilled me more than the winter air. I was stunned into silence for a moment. I only met Zhou once, but I felt as if I had lost someone very close. In December of last year, during my second visit to China, on the evening before our departure for Tokyo, I gave a modest dinner party for the Chinese friends who had been of assistance to us. At the conclusion of the dinner, I was told that, in spite of his illness, Zhou Enlai was eager to see us.

At about ten o'clock one evening, we went to the hospital where he had kindly come to the entrance hall to await us. He greeted me smilingly with a handshake and the remark, "Since my health is better now, I felt that I must see you."

When I had visited China six months earlier, he had been too ill to have visitors. Now he said he was improving. But to our shock and sorrow, his illness was cancer. The moderate improvement he felt at the time was probably the psychological strength and courage of a leader who had braved long years of hardship and toil and whose intrepid qualities and great kindness gleamed together like a light in his eyes. After a photograph of the whole group was taken to commemorate the occasion, the interview with my wife and me took place in one of the hospital rooms.

With a prayer for his recovery, I said, "For the sake of the eight hundred million people of China, I hope you will regain your health and remain in good physical condition for many years to come." I still recall the courtesy with which he acknowledged my wish.

Two things discussed that evening left a deep impression on me. One was Zhou Enlai's conviction that the remaining quarter of this century is going to be of the most tremendous importance for all humanity. The other was the nostalgia and affection he expressed for Japan and his wish that relations between our countries could go beyond mere governmental amity. He remarked that over fifty years ago, when he had left Japan, the cherries had been in bloom. His reply to my invitation to come again when the trees were in flower was a doubt that such a wish could be realized. I suspect he knew then that the lamp of his life was burning low. Previously he had always told Japanese visitors of his eagerness to again see old familiar places in their country. He was responsible for overcoming the hard feelings left by the Sino-Japanese war and for reestablishing relations between our two nations. I very strongly wanted him to enjoy the cherries in their pride and glory once again.

When I visited Beijing four months later, Zhou Enlai's condition had deteriorated. Vice Premier Deng Xiaoping told me at the time that great care was being taken of Zhou and that he was being spared all official worries. On this trip, I took a painting of cherries in full bloom that I had commissioned a young artist to do. I hoped that Zhou Enlai could at least vicariously experience the flowers' splendor. I entrusted the picture to Liao Chengzhi, chairman of the China-Japan Friendship Association.

As another gesture of respect, I suggested planting the Zhou Cherry on the grounds of Soka University. The tree, which was set in place by Japanese students with the help of visiting Chinese students, is now shaking its branches against the winter winds but will bloom at last when spring comes.

I remember a single old cherry tree that, surviving the ravages of war to stand alone in a burned-out part of Tokyo, gave heart to everyone who saw it. My long-standing fondness for cherry trees has led me to have many of them planted in several parts of the country. But the Zhou Cherry has a special place in my heart. Spring or winter, for me it will always bloom as a symbol of future generations of friendship between China and Japan.

I was attending a meeting of about a thousand people in Kyoto when word came of Zhou Enlai's death. We included a prayer for his repose in the premeeting services. Then, when official news arrived from Beijing, we learned of the deep grief of the entire Chinese nation, and also of the touching tribute his wife made to him in the form of a meter-long, handwritten banner bearing the words "Zhou Enlai, Battle Comrade" and signed "In Sorrow, Xiao Chao."

Xiao Chao, or Little Chao, is the affectionate name Zhou Enlai used for his wife Deng Yingchao, who was always a great assistance to him in his work. The two words *Battle Comrade* symbolize the fifty years these two people spent together sharing the love and trust that warmed them in the cold and hardships of the struggle to accomplish the Chinese revolution. They were married when he was twenty-seven and she was twenty-three and thereafter helped and cared for each other as true battle comrades. In happier times, when asked the secret of his health and vigor, Zhou Enlai used to say that it was his having given himself entirely to the revolution.

Many people in many parts of the world mourn the loss in Zhou Enlai of one of the greatest leaders of the twentieth century. Personally, I have fond memories of him, but the most impressive is that of a man of unbending faith and lofty devotion, which enabled him to abandon self and live solely for his people.

Daisaku Ikeda

A Smile, a Hand, a Fallen Star

January 23, 1976

On the eighth of January, the day on which you left for the Kyoto-Osaka area, I departed for four days and three nights on Okinawa, where I visited the ruins of some old castles, saw the Ocean Exposition buildings, enjoyed the beauty of the sea and felt deeply touched by the sites of the tragic battles of Okinawa during World War II. I have not been there for sixteen years, but I shall share my impressions of Okinawa with you in greater detail later.

I was interested to learn that the city of Osaka is important in the period of your youth that, though partly gloomy and difficult, must have been filled with enthusiasm and passion and certainly helped develop you as you are today.

The twelve or thirteen years I spent working as a newspaper man in Osaka during my thirties and forties span the period of World War II. After the war, when I was already in my middle forties, I returned to Tokyo and began writing novels. The experiences I had in Osaka were the foundation of my life as a novelist. Of the many things I saw and did there, nothing made as great an impression on me as the sight of the burned city at the end of the war. It seems like only yesterday when on the day of defeat, I finished a story for the social page, left the newspaper offices and wandered absent-mindedly among the ruins. Thirty years have passed since then.

Although I go to nearby Kyoto and Nara several times yearly, since I came to Tokyo to live, I have visited Osaka rarely and then only when I had some special reason. It is not that I lack fond memories of the city where I spent many of my younger years. I recall the city, the people and their distinctive way of talking with great affection. But I want to retain my image of the ruined city with as much unaltered power and clarity as possible. I am a little embarrassed to admit I have deliberately avoided Osaka for a reason connected with my work, but such is the case. I intend someday to write a novel based on my experiences there during the five or six years during and immediately after the war and therefore must not disturb my recollections. Fortunately, the fairly detailed diaries I kept can serve as a basis on which to reconstruct this dark time in Japanese history. The material in these diaries is of the greatest importance to me, especially since I was in my prime when I wrote them. As a writer I am obliged to put this material to use. But I know that I cannot write the book without putting my whole self into it. It will be a difficult task, as will be choosing the correct time to release it. For all of these reasons, it is important for me to keep in my mind's eye a clear picture of the scorched ruins, the black market and the other hardships of Osaka as it was then, until I have finished the book.

I too have long wanted to visit the chateau where Leonardo da Vinci lived his final years. When I wrote a short essay about him last year, I felt uneasy about not having made the trip to see the room where he died. The main theme of the piece, which was called *Hohoemi to te to* (The smile, the hand, and . . .), was my attempt to examine the significance "Mona Lisa," "Saint John the Baptist" and "Saint Anne," three paintings that were in his room when he died, had for Leonardo at the close of his life. The title of the essay refers to the mysterious Mona Lisa smile and the wonderful upraised hand of John the Baptist. In my interpretation, the smile and the hand constitute a farewell to the artist's life of sorrow, irony and anger. The painting of Saint Anne reveals a pure and lofty peace unlike anything conceivable on this earth. Leonardo probably entertained contrasting feelings consonant with the contrasting moods of the three pictures. Though forced to undergo the sadness and irony of having to abandon his homeland, he did not break under the strain but instead dreamed of the bliss hinted at in the painting of Saint Anne.

Perhaps, if I had been able to visit the chateau and the room where Leonardo lived at the end, some parts of my personal version of his final state of mind might have been expanded or altered. Among the three impressive sentences you found engraved on a copper tablet in the chateau, the last moves me most deeply: "A full life gives a tranquil death." I am certain this statement is especially applicable to artists who have lived full lives. I intend to be in Europe for a brief while this winter and, if my busy schedule permits, should like to visit the chateau.

Like you, I felt as if I had lost someone close when I heard the news of the death of Zhou Enlai, though there was, of course, no intimacy between him and me. I met him for the first time during a trip to China in 1961 when a group of writers was granted an interview for about an hour in the Great Hall of the People in Beijing. We discussed literature. Zhou Enlai praised the *Dream of the Red Chamber*, and when he spoke of Genghis Khan in some connection, referred to him as the "blue wolf" in reference to a novel of mine by that title. I doubt he had read the book. He was probably only being courteous to his guests.

I met him for the second time in 1963 at celebrations to mark the one thousand and two hundredth year since the death of the great Buddhist priest and missionary to Japan Jianzhen [Ganjin in Japanese]. The ceremonies were held at both Beijing and Yangzhou. The group with which I was traveling had an interview with Zhou Enlai in the chambers over the Tien'an-men gate on the day after the national celebration. At that time a book of mine called *Tempyō no Iraka* (*The Roof Tile of Tempyo*) had just been published in Chinese translation. Even in the confusion of shaking hands with everyone present, Zhou found time to say a word or two about my book and to ask what I was writing then.

I saw him for the third time last year at a national banquet in China. He arrived a little late. Seeing him from a distance, I could tell that his health was failing and that there was cause to worry about his attending such a dinner. These three meetings were all the contacts I ever had with him, but at each encounter Zhou Enlai impressed me as a very courteous, kindly person whose death was justifiably compared in a recent newspaper article to the falling of a great star.

I mentioned my trip to Okinawa at the beginning of this letter. The days our group spent there were few, but truly rewarding. With paved highways in both the north and south and with modern bypasses, the bright, new tourist-oriented Okinawa is entirely different from the war-scarred, gloomy island that I saw sixteen years ago on my only other visit. Though it is a favorite tourist spot, its isolation from the main Japanese islands now prevents its being, and will probably prevent its becoming, a noisy, crowded tourist trap. This is as I want it to be, for in the light of the tragedy suffered there in World War II, Okinawa is a special island and should be a quiet place of prayers for peace.

Though it was the first of January, a species of cherry bloomed in the mountains and yellow rape flowered around the villages. We drove along the seacoast almost daily, and, when I visited the buildings of the Ocean Exposition and saw the waters and the coral reefs, I understood why the sea there is described as seven colored.

I was guided through the remains and sites of a number of Okinawan castles, whose exact construction dates are unknown but which are thought to have been destroyed by fire in the fifteenth and sixteenth centuries. Excavations of the sites are currently under way. Though I have little knowledge of ancient Okinawan history, these excursions led me to think there must have been places for worship of the gods all over the island. Okinawa must have been virtually an island of prayer. I went to Sēfā-utaki, the holiest of places for the Ryukyuans and saw the island of Kudaka, which is said to be the place of origin of the local gods and which is worshipped only from afar.

The days since my return from Okinawa have been cold. But this morning, as I walked in my little garden, I discovered buds on one branch each of the red and white plum trees and still larger ones on the red azalea. The plants are preparing for spring. But it is still a long way off.

Yasushi Inoue

The Blessedness of Being Taught

February 17, 1976

Last week I spied a small white flower in the garden. Today, when I went outdoors, I saw that, here and there, the white plum was blooming, about ten days earlier than usual.

For some time now, I have been inordinately fond of the period when these trees flower. I wait for the blooms to come and feel sad when they drop. Though the air is still wintry cold, I have the feeling spring is quietly waiting just out of sight for the time to make an appearance.

On the day I discovered the first plum blossom, I left for Kyoto to hold meetings about a publication project I have agreed to supervise. Our work was over in a single evening, and for the rest of my stay, I had the first chance in many years to enjoy Kyoto in February, the month when the city is at its best. In March, the tourists flock in. But in the middle of February, Kyotoites have their city to themselves. Immediately recognizable as natives, they stroll their own streets in their own distinctive way.

I lived in Kyoto while I was in college and for many years after graduation and nearly until the end of World War II. At that time I moved to Osaka, but previously I had commuted daily between Kyoto and the Osaka offices of the *Mainichi Shimbun*, where I worked. My job as a journalist brought me to Kyoto once or twice weekly to visit the university or to call on artists and scholars.

As I walked around the city on my recent visit, I realized how many of the friends and acquaintances I made in those days—how many of those artists and scholars who were kind to me, who touched me in one way or another, and who did much that was important in forming the

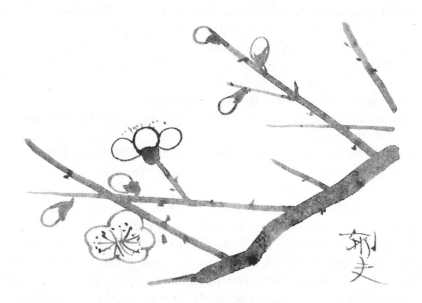

person I have become—have now departed from this world. Many of them died before I could express my gratitude to them. My wife's parents and our second daughter, who died shortly after birth, are laid to rest in Kyoto. Perhaps more of my dead friends are there in such places as the cemeteries of the Chionin and Hōnenin temples than anywhere else. And, this time, I felt that though many living friends surround me, the dead friends with me are no fewer in number.

For the first time, my three-day stay made me reflect deeply on the truth that, though for longer or shorter times, all human beings live their allotted spans and then must make way for others. The process of making way goes on constantly, without surcease. Only this past year, three people with whom I was once on close terms died in Kyoto. But I have the special privilege of the living: to remember.

As a young unknown journalist, whenever I went to Kyoto I would think up an excuse to call at the Gojō-zaka studio of ceramist Kanjirō Kawai, who always treated me as an equal. "I've found something really wonderful! Here. What do you think of it?" With a remark like this he would set before me a piece of Okinawan pottery or a vessel from no one knows where and add, "Now you must admit there's nothing much finer than this!" And miraculously the object he was showing me appeared to be truly fine in my eyes. Mr. Kawai would proceed to explain just what was outstanding about the piece and go on, in his infective and enthusiastic way, to relate his feelings upon discovering it and how it had come into his possession. From start to finish, he talked about the beautiful object he had found. Sometimes the conversation never veered from this one topic.

He taught me that I must see things with my own eyes. For me, he was less the central figure in the folk-pottery movement founded by him and Muneyoshi Yanagi [1889–1961] and Shōji Hamada than my own private coach in aesthetic appreciation. From him I learned what an artist is and what beauty is.

I visited him several times after becoming a novelist. I recall once asking him to sell me a work of his that stood in a corner of the studio. At first he seemed reluctant to part with the piece, then, standing in front of it, he said, "Well, friend, do you want to go to stay with Mr. Inoue?" precisely as if he were speaking to a living person. I was of course delighted to acquire one of Mr. Kawai's works but much more thrilled to learn the kind of relation that existed between him and the things he made.

He died in 1966, at the age of seventy-six, and his studio has been converted into a memorial museum. It is scarcely surprising that many people visit it daily, since it houses not only his own works but also a large number of those things that his discerning eye labeled beautiful.

The year before his death, he drew up a set of self-guidelines, which I am convinced actually did guide him in daily life in his studio.

> Live according to the great Law of heaven and earth.
> Revere and respect that Law.
> Live with others in respectful amity.
> Be aware always that the self and the other are one.
> Realize that you are the most immature of all people.
> Respect poverty and return to simplicity.
> Reproach yourself before reproaching others.
> Constantly confront a new you.
> Make answer to the world of the infinite.
> Attempt to discover a more wonderful self.

I majored in aesthetics at Kyoto University, but in name only. I rarely attended class and understandably did not enjoy the favor of my principal teacher, Professor Juzō Ueda. But after graduation, as a journalist, I frequently had opportunities to call on him at his home, which was then in the Komatsubara district. I did not really get to know him until then. The neatness and cleanliness of everything around him struck me especially. Whenever I called, he always greeted me, seated in perfect propriety, listened quietly to my remarks, and then replied impeccably, point by point. I thought then that this was the way people should treat each other.

After the death of his wife, he moved to the home of his married daughter in Suita, where he had a small study of his own, apart from the main house. In this room he devoted himself to writing on aesthetics and aesthetics history until his death at more than eighty years of age. I called on him from time to time after I had become a novelist. Seeing him at his desk, I was always impressed with the idea of observing a scholar completely devoid of relations with the ordinary world.

The year before his death, together with the last letter I ever had from him, I received an extract of one of his articles. The letter was encouraging comment on some of my work that he had read. It contained no mention of the article, which was a short criticism of the Leonardo da Vinci "Annunciation," stating that the picture has faults, and may be a fake.

I was taken aback. I had written and published a poem in praise of the picture and realized at once that, in sending me this criticism, Professor Ueda was silently telling me that he and I disagreed and that I should read what he had to say for my own information.

I did read it and was made aware that my praise of the work had been based on nothing but my own instincts. Professor Ueda pointed out the carelessness of such an attitude toward a work of art.

I discussed the matter with Shūji Takashina, who investigated and found out that although at one time the "Annunciation" was called a spurious work and is still considered a fake by some, it is now recognized as genuine and even a masterpiece. I did not have to revise my enthusiastic appraisal, but people had once doubted the very authenticity of the picture, and it had been slovenly of a novelist to publish unhesitating, fervent admiration for a work without so much as finding out whether it is genuine.

Professor had corrected me for the last time, gently, without a sound. I realized what blessings my teachers have been.

Yasushi Inoue

Early Spring, the Spirit of Prayer

February 19, 1976

Since the beginning of the year, while you were enjoying a few tranquil days in Kyoto, I have traveled to Fukuoka, Kagoshima, Osaka, Nara, Kyoto and Aichi Prefecture. The poet Matsuo Bashō [1644–94] was a great traveler, and though the convenience of modern transportation, tight schedules and my own personality prevent my savoring the elegance and charm of leisurely journeys like his, I at least share with him an obsession for movement.

The plum trees in your garden hinted at spring for you—ten days early this year. For me, the breath of early spring and memories associated with it arrived in the form of a large display of wild flowers and grasses brought into the lobby of the culture center of our organization in Fukuoka, on the island of Kyushu, one of the places I visited. In a patch of earth, about three square meters in area, our Fukuoka members had carefully and with great expenditure of patience and time set such familiar but—in the urban environment at any rate—increasingly rare plants as butterbur, horsetail, pale primroses and daisies, which lightened and gladdened the hearts of their visitors, including me.

Looking at them, I recalled lying long ago sunk in new grass with arms and legs spread wide, allowing the warmth of the spring sun in the infinite sky overhead and of the quickening earth under me to seep into my body. Perhaps the glories of spring are more overwhelming in the sweeping landscapes one can still enjoy only a few minutes' drive from such capitals as Paris and Moscow, but this small indoor patch of earth and wild plants carried the same spring message, reinforced by the affection of the people who devoted time and effort to create it.

Such people represent for me the kind of warm concern and caring that remind me of the poetry of early spring and that always cause me to wonder when, if ever, I shall meet again the people whose company I am enjoying at the moment. In most instances, the desire for further encounter and acquaintance persists, but given the uncertainty of human life, all we can do is pray that separation will not be final.

This is as it should be, since at the deepest level, prayer is man's way of giving direct, unvarnished expression to the thought and state of mind of the moment. It is unique in man and has been one of his patterns of behavior since before organized religions existed. Neanderthal man is said to have known how to pray.

In spite of many signs of increasing interest in religion, however, in the modern world, prayer, while becoming formalized and a prominent part of religious ceremonies, has lost its place in the daily lives of large numbers of people. This is regrettable.

The act of praying constitutes recognition of some greater, absolute reality and symbolizes entrusting the self to that reality. It further indicates a willingness to be humble and to attempt to refine and develop one's better potentialities further. Prayer and the faith from which it springs are the most independent of human attributes. Entrusting it to absolute reality through prayer manifests the self and simultaneously self-transformation, from self-centeredness to compassionate altruism.

Prayer is important to the religious organization to which I belong. It helps us attain our double goal of generating within our group consideration and compassion and then of contributing to the creation of a happier world by extending this consideration and compassion beyond the confines of our group. Prayer can sublimate ugliness, which, together with beauty, is part of the bewildering diversity of all life, and can stimulate the creation of compassionate values.

The small indoor plot of grasses and wild flowers prepared for their guests by the members of our Fukuoka branch did more than brighten the eye with hints of spring: it represented the spirit of concern for others and of compassion that is part of the spirit of the innate human act of prayer.

Daisaku Ikeda

Graduations, Commencements

Here in Okayama, where I have come after attending the first graduation ceremonies of the Soka Girls' School in Osaka, cherries are in full bloom. I disagree with the general Japanese interpretation of the appeal of these flowers. I do not prize them for the suddenness of their blooming and the evanescence of their glory, which ends while still at its peak. Instead, I love the cherries because, yearly, when spring comes, they burst forth in a splendor of pink, beautiful color revealing the vibrant force of life that has been active in them throughout the cold and winds of winter.

I suppose the people who recently have been claiming that there is no need to hold ceremonies to mark the opening of school careers or graduation ceremonies to celebrate their conclusion have their reasons. But I cannot agree with them. It is refreshing and stimulating to remember the points that divide life as the changing of the seasons does.

I have decided to make education my ultimate undertaking. A revolution in education can change human beings on a deeper plane than economic or political revolutions. Of course, just as the will to improve himself in human terms on the part of the instructor and the personality and humanity emerging from these efforts are primary in education, so the human revolution is the main preliminary condition for a revolution in education.

Ideal for the time when a group of young people commemorate the starting point of their adult lives, graduation day was fair, the rain of the preceding night having stopped. The sun shone brightly on the washed trees, and—as the school founder—I rejoiced.

Naturally, in connection with this graduation and with that of the Soka High School in Tokyo, where I am to deliver the final address, I gave thought to optimum relations between graduating students and their alma mater—their spiritual and intellectual hometown. Everyone is nostalgic about his alma mater, but this emotion, oriented to the past, has little positive effect on human actions. In the message I have been writing for the Tokyo Soka High School, I attempt to leave the graduating class with the thought that if their school is part of the very ground of their spirits, it will be a positive, progressive influence on them for the rest of their lives, helping them, in spite of their youth, to cultivate discernment as fine as that of any adult.

I was most deeply moved by the sense of gratitude and affection the younger girls displayed for their graduating older sisters. Every window in the classroom building was hung with banners and posters expressing congratulatory sentiments. The corridors along which the graduates passed, diplomas in hand, on their way from the ceremonies had been diligently polished by the other students, as if to say goodby with as much luster as possible. All the graduating girls wore pink paper roses made by the younger girls, who also decorated the welcome arch at the entrance to the grounds, and this demonstration of affection seemed to be only the natural, grateful outcome of wholesome relations in the preceding years at school.

In my address to the graduating class, I tried to stress the importance of an upright and outstanding personality and told the girls that this was something not to be learned from theories but to be acquired through the personal contacts and experiences they had shared with fellow students.

Women are often so concerned with getting married and raising families that their viewpoints and personalities narrow until they see only their own happiness and that of the people close to them. In an effort to prevent the Soka Girls' School students from falling into this state, three years ago, when this graduating class was entering school— the cherries were in flower then too—I tried to instill in them the idea that it is impossible to build one's happiness on the unhappiness of others and that a broad approach to life is essential. My admonition alone was not enough to have the desired effect on them: an education system with heart, as well as the individual efforts of each girl, was required.

I think the attitude of the principal Mitsuo Makino shows that the first of these elements is assured. When the photographer Jun Miki came to take some pictures of the campus, he wrote a note, which is now one of the memorabilia of the graduating class displayed in the long passageway connecting the campus buildings. Miki said that when he arrived at the school, at eight thirty in the morning, the principal was standing at the gate greeting students. Miki wanted to take a picture of the scene but could not get a satisfactory shot of all faces showing at the same time, since the principal always bowed before the girls bowed. I have learned that Principal Makino meets the girls at the gate every morning and has done so daily for the past three years.

By showing courteous concern for his charges and in overcoming all the difficulties of his task, Mr. Makino illustrates something else, I told the girls at their graduation ceremony. Today much talk is devoted to the proper placement of the average level in educational planning. In a class of fifty or sixty, there are bound to be a few at the top, a few at the bottom, and a large middle sector. Where should the average level be? If it is too low, the outstanding students will be bored, but if it is too high, the slow students will be lost entirely. I told the girls that the outstanding must accept the lower setting of average and then look out for themselves. They need less help than slow students. The things they find easy present no problems, and if they are truly outstanding, they will not give in to subjects they find difficult, as their principal Mr. Makino does not give in even to the difficulty of standing at the school gate every morning.

When school is over, even in this day of rapid social change, most women live similar lives and face similar hardships. They generally get married and have children. Unknown troubles lie in store for them. Some are widowed at an early age; some find life with their husbands so unpleasant that divorce is the only answer. Some have children with serious mental or physical defects. Men find support in business or professional lives. For women, however, there is no support outside the home. And they must have self-confidence and strength, since they are themselves the major support of the family.

In a previous letter I spoke of my trip to Kyushu and of my meeting an inspiring old woman. One of her experiences during World War II illustrates the kind of independence women must have—the kind of independence our educational systems must give them. In the heat of August, in the final months of the war, when she was a collector for the local post office, some American prisoners were being forced to dig airraid shelters not far from her place of work. One of them, suffering from intense thirst, came to a nearby well and, after laboriously drawing water in a bottle, started to drink. Another woman came along and shouted, "We haven't got any water to give the likes of you!" then snatched the bottle from him and poured its contents on the ground. The woman of whom I am speaking suddenly thought that perhaps her own husband in Burma, a soldier doomed to die in battle before long, might be thirsty in the heat of summer in a foreign land, with no one to give him a drink. She quickly drew more water, followed the American who was about to return to work and put the full bottle in the grass by the roadside where he could get it. With a silent bow of gratitude, he gulped the water down.

Gradually, drawing water for the prisoners became an unofficial daily duty for her. And, if many of her compatriots looked at her with animosity in their eyes, the Americans always bowed in gratitude when she went by.

She was not in the wrong. The American prisoners were not in the wrong. It was war that was wrong. The attempt to make people fight and die in the name of a national state was wrong. And this woman had the strength and independence of character to stand up against her neighbors and to do the thing she knew was right.

To give our young women this kind of independence of thought and action, an education revolution is needed. Not a revolution of curricula, financing or politics, but a human revolution reaching to the depths of the heart of every individual human being involved.

Daisaku Ikeda

Boldness from Sunlight

March 25, 1976

The cherries are blooming in Okayama, where you were when you wrote me last, and a few days ago it was warm enough here in Tokyo to convince me that spring was right around the corner. Then the temperature dropped. The erratic flow of cold air over the Japanese islands at this time of year always teases us with a few warm days, allowing us to think that springtime has come; then sudden cold snaps plunge us back into winter. There are interesting words in the Japanese language for these sharp cold disappointments: *haruzamu* (spring cold) or *hanabie* (flower–chill), which stands especially for those cold days that strike in April, when the cherries, the greatest glory of the Japanese spring, are already in flower. But in spite of unpredictable temperature fluctuations, all the plants know their order and bloom and fade in established succession without being much disturbed by chill in the midst of balmy days. In my little garden, for instance, where I walked a few minutes before returning to my study to go on with this letter, the red and white plums have long since faded and fallen and the apricots have passed their prime. The sweet daphne is in full bloom, while the heavy purple lilacs, the small late-flowering plum, the tiny spirea and the red azaleas are just beginning to bud. Each species blooms and then relinquishes the stage to its successor until the process culminates in the cherries.

Since this year in late February, just at the blooming time of the plums, I made a busy trip to Europe, I am all the more grateful for the gentleness and beauty of Japanese spring. This was my first experience with European winter. I went prepared for severe cold, but in London,

Stockholm and Hamburg, the temperatures were no lower than they were here when I returned. In fact, people everywhere said this has been the warmest European winter in years.

In Hamburg, I was told that the sun practically never appears in winter. We had one sunny day, to my surprise; then the gray, sunless gloom returned to cover the city. It did not rain, and it did not snow. But the idea of a whole winter without the bright sunlight is depressing. From my hotel lobby window I could see women, bulky with thick, warm clothes, all leaning the same way as if by prearrangement, and walking the cobbled streets. Perhaps they were not thinking of anything in particular, but to me it seemed each woman was engrossed in her own isolated thoughts as she plodded her heavy way. Not only in Hamburg, but in Stockholm as well, everyone seemed to be enduring the winter in quiet anticipation of spring and the sun.

I could not help thinking how comfortable the Japanese winter is. As long as it is not raining or snowing, no matter how cold, the sun usually shines bright. I suspect this is in a way responsible for the sense of energy I felt when observing groups of young Japanese tourists all over Europe. Perhaps what I felt flowing from these people was less energy than the boldness of a people long accustomed to a climate like ours.

Living in a totally different climate undoubtedly has a sobering effect. In the several speeches I delivered under the sponsorship of Kodansha, the publishing house, and Japan Air Lines, I found that all of the Japanese members of the audience were very serious. They asked sensible questions when my talks were finished and displayed none of the mild rowdiness always permitted in similar situations in Japan. I came to the conclusion that living and working for a long time in a different natural environment must make Japanese people more thoughtful about life, human nature, faith and their own country. Probably sharp differences in climate, customs and life-styles create serious problems for such people.

Filled with glad anticipation of our gentle spring, I returned to Japan only to be shocked by the Lockheed scandals, which have the entire nation in a stir and which must cause Japanese living overseas intense perplexity and anguish.

But for the graduates of the Soka Girls' School, this spring must have

been both bright and special. What with a fine guide like you and an outstanding principal like Mr. Makino, whether they go into ordinary society or continue pursuing their education in some institute of higher learning, these young ladies will always recall this spring season. I thank you for sharing their commencement excercises with me.

In my recollections too there are a number of special springtimes. For instance, I shall never forget the sunlight falling through the trees in Kenroku Park, in the city of Kanazawa, the spring of the year I entered Kanazawa University. The Tang-period Chinese poet Meng Jiao wrote about the spring wind and the hoofs of his horse as, on the day when, already an old man, he finally passed examinations for the official third degree—something like a modern doctorate—and spent hours looking at the flowers of the city of Chang'an.

The flowers of Chang'an were peonies, not cherries; and the poem conjures up an image of a sun-drenched old man on horseback, not of a young man, as I was in Kanazawa, or of young women, like your Soka Girls' School graduates. Nonetheless, in all three instances, a stage in education either started or successfully finished made a certain day unique.

In 1937, while many of my comrades were still battling on the Asian mainland, I was being treated in an army hospital in Osaka to which I had been sent after I contracted an illness. Early in April, when an unforgettable sun, peaceful and unrelated to warring, shone down on me, I was released from the hospital. Realizing many of my companions were still in danger, I could not enjoy the season without some compunction. But I could experience spring, and the experience became something I shall always remember.

Still another unforgettable spring occurred in 1946, immediately after World War II. The sun then shone on scars of war, on mobs of repatriated soldiers, and on the desperate doings of the black market. It was a time when the value of money fluctuated daily and when there was never enough to eat or to wear. A sick Japan and a sick Japanese people, daily reading in the newspapers—at least in Osaka, where I was—words like *liberty*, for which no one as yet had any real use, or *humanism*, which seemed flimsy to us, were suddenly bathed in spring sunlight that made even that empty time indelibly memorable.

I felt something very strong when I learned you are resolved to make education your ultimate undertaking. I was also impressed with the strength in your statement that a revolution in education can change human beings on a deeper plane than revolutions in economics or politics. I am not at home in the fields of politics and economics. I lack confidence to discuss those chimerical, vast, mysterious powers that can change human beings for better or worse. But in connection with education, I have a great dream. Though educators are probably now grappling with many difficulties related to Japanese education, undesirable phenomena in the field nonetheless emerge.

One of the most serious is the emphasis on the examinations that consume too much of the life of young children in a system in which advancement from class to class and school to school is considered of the greatest importance. Certainly the system results in the selection of a small number of elite students, but this causes all the others to feel shut out of this elite circle. Unfortunately, many young people today entertain the mistaken notion that getting into a good school sets them up for life. The very word *elite* has an insincere, unpleasant ring.

Tests and the hardships associated with them begin as early as primary school. Small children are sent to special schools for coaching, or tutors are hired to help them at home. I feel very sorry when I see little girls and boys having to study under such conditions. But all parents agree that this kind of thing must be done.

I believe that spiritual contacts between the teacher and the taught—relations of the kind that you have long been conducting—are essential to any education that deserves the name. Cannot something be done about our modern universities in which knowledge is bought and sold?

Yasushi Inoue

Criteria for the Future

April 14, 1976

The cherry blossoms have all fallen, and though the weather remains cloudy and cold, I anticipate a leap over spring directly into early summer. Our correspondence has now come the full course of a year—spring, summer, autumn and winter. Whereas you, as usual, have been busy and productive, I have not finished a single full-scale work. The creative writer may be in a somewhat special position in this respect; still my failure to be able to announce to you the completion of my novel on Sen no Rikyū does embarrass me. I am not even halfway through.

Four or five days ago, however, in Kyoto, I had an opportunity to examine a large collection of tea ceremony utensils once owned and used by Rikyū. The display was extremely illuminating in that it hinted at the true nature of the man. The abundant documentary material on him produces a vague image. But the black or red-glazed tea bowls he actually used brought me closer to his mind. The bowls, scoops, tea containers, vases and other articles he selected are simple and unaffected, yet they are the very standards of excellence for all such things. I have always examined Rikyū's tea utensils with great interest when the chance arose. But usually I have seen them only in small numbers. It is of the greatest importance to be able to examine a large number of them at one time. Doing so at the exhibition in Kyoto made it clear to me that he was too frank and unpretentious to have anything in common with the adulation and virtual deification that are often heaped on him.

I am frequently asked exactly what I want to write about Sen no

Rikyū. I shall concentrate on the refined, somber tea ceremony he founded and guided and on its relation with its tempestuous historical period—the so-called Period of the Nation at War [1482–1558]—and the undercurrents. I doubt that the beverage—tea—alone possessed the power to fascinate the minds of leading warriors at a time so insecure that life itself was often in danger. I should like to know what these men found in the tea ceremony that compelled them to isolate themselves from pressing affairs and sit for hours in the very special space known as the tea ceremony room.

Isolated from the everyday world, the tea ceremony room is a microcosm to itself, with its own distinctive value criteria. The man of political authority must be deprived of it during the time he is in this space. He must fit himself into the value system in which modesty, simplicity and beauty dominate. Secular concerns are abandoned, and the tea bowl and other carefully selected utensils on the *tatami* mats are lords of the space. Participants in the ceremony sit in front of the bowl and engage in conversations divorced from practical society. As he sat in such rooms preparing bowls of green tea and entertaining the military commanders of the nations, what thoughts did Sen no Rikyū entertain?

He is said to have died at the age of seventy or seventy-one. At that late stage in life, probably death was on his mind from time to time. But he was not to be allowed to die naturally. Instead, Toyotomi Hideyoshi, the military ruler of the land, commanded Sen no Rikyū to kill himself. It would have been possible for Rikyū to appeal for clemency but he did not. What forced him to reject this way out and settle for imposed suicide? These are the issues on which I want to concentrate in my novel. To make the book convincing, I shall have to delve into the religious aspects of the tea ceremony. At present, all of this is wrapped in mist, but it will become clearer as I continue writing.

As a special space, the tea ceremony room survives intact today. Other kinds of special spaces, however, are being violated in one way or another. For instance, the hospital. In days gone by, hospitals were distinctive spaces demanding special quiet ways of walking and behaving on the part of doctors and nurses. Patients too moved in ways that made it obvious what they were. Now all this has changed. Not long ago, I called on an ill friend in a large urban hospital. The lobby was packed with people waiting to see doctors. A baseball game was being shown on a television set. A loud-speaker system was constantly paging patients or doctors. Many of the visitors had brought their children, who contributed to the general bustle and noise. With the outside world pushing its way right into the hospital, it was almost inconceivable that somewhere in this crowded, lively building, people were battling with fatal sicknesses. It seems to me that even in the largest general hospitals visitors should adopt an attitude and style of behavior in keeping with the nature of an institution devoted to caring for the sick. The staff of the hospital too must evolve policies to ensure maintenance of the proper mood.

The hotel in Japan is another special space that has lost its individuality. In Europe, the hotel is the domain of the guest. Although it is not necessarily wrong, it is regrettable that Japanese hotel lobbies have been converted into extensions of the street or into waiting rooms, bars, coffee shops and shopping arcades.

Other places too suggest the deindividualization of special spaces. It is hard to find in Japan today parks that are quiet and safe enough for elderly people to stroll in. Even the family living room is transformed into something strange by the television left running constantly. I should like to see individuality and proper moods restored to a number of spaces like the ones I have mentioned, but, in the present society of movement and change, I probably shall not get my wish.

In my letter to you in February, I spoke of my loss at the deaths of Juzō Ueda and Kanjirō Kawai, both of whom gave me a great deal. Recently, I have been saddened by the passing of another respected senior, Kichijirō Inoue, under whom I was trained in the Osaka offices of the *Mainichi Shimbun*. He ordered me to take over the art column, thus compelling me to study art, both new and old. Later he insisted I take charge of the religion column, which entailed commenting on classical works on the subject. Thanks to his instruction and guidance I came to appreciate the Buddhist classics as a wide range of literary expression including essays, drama and theses.

More a scholar than a newspaperman, Mr. Inoue wrote on sociology, had degrees and actually taught at universities. As a younger man, I found working under him very trying.

For a while he made me go with him to look at the ancient Buddhist temples in Nara every Sunday. At the time, I considered it a burdensome duty. I have since become very grateful to him for it. He was uninterested in any Buddhist statue or painting that was not absolutely first class. He guided me, and it was on his instructions that I began to sign myself as a critic of modern art. For a young newspaperman, this kind of thing posed a grave responsibility. To prepare myself better, at Mr. Inoue's prompting, I signed up for a graduate course in the art department of Kyoto University, intending to combine additional education with my duties as a reporter and columnist. Actually, I did little more than take some books out of the school library.

Mr. Inoue tolerated no laxness in my writing. I recall now that if he found something of mine unsatisfactory, he would merely remark, "Well, we can't have anything like this. Can we?" I met him only once or twice after I became a novelist. Perhaps during my forties and fifties, when I was extremely busy, I may have been afraid to see him. Just as in the days when I worked for the newspaper, he might have read something and then said, "Well, we can't have anything like this. Can we?" About four or five years ago, I had one long talk with him.

He was nearly eighty at the time. Although he spoke only favorably of my works, this did not eliminate my reserve or completely cure my fear of what he might say.

When the retired emperor Toba died, in 1156, the poet Saigyō said, "At last, tonight, profound friend, I know the profundity of your friendship." Upon hearing of Mr. Inoue's death, I recalled this verse. A valued, special senior friend had vanished from the earth. I had not thanked him as he deserved. And another regret was added to my life, which is already too full of regrets.

We have been corresponding for a year now, and I am very grateful to you for the many valuable things you have said to me. But I regret I have not always responded to your comments as satisfactorily as I might have. Nonetheless, I am happy to have had the chance to express my thoughts openly and frankly to you in letter form once monthly.

You are a very active man with heavy responsibilities. Still I request that you continue making contributions to the creation of a better future, in which such qualities as simplicity, modesty, beauty and strength—the criteria on which Sen no Rikyū judged tea ceremony utensils—will play a leading role.

Yasushi Inoue

The Season of Humanization

April 19, 1976

I read your emotion-filled twelfth letter while in the city of Sapporo, on the northern island of Hokkaido. Since I move about constantly, I have become accustomed to thinking as I travel and writing as I think. The leisure to meditate in peace and calm that I used to dream of when a young man is now a remote thing. Each time I receive a letter from you, I feel I have come into immediate touch with your emotions and have gained a deeper understanding of you as a person and of your work. I have attempted to put the things I have gained from you to use in my activities and to bring them to the members of our organization. If possible, I should like for us to be companions in many things, including the activities in which I participate. No matter what you write, you speak for yourself. To be frank, I should like to say that, each month as I have read your letters—your revelations of your own vital life—I have felt the deepest involvement. In them I have intuitively perceived literature. You have allowed me to see the soul of a writer who is engrossed in sublimation toward humanity.

This trip to Hokkaido is my first in a long time. On April 16, in the Hitsujigaoka hills on the outskirts of Sapporo, the Soka Kindergarten, the first such institution founded by our organization, was officially opened. As the founder, I was invited to attend.

The natural setting of the school, with Mount Moiwa and a range of snow-capped mountains in the distance and with fertile fields in the foreground, is ideal for the education of young children. This site was chosen because of the significance of the environment to the initiation of a course of education. At present, the butterburs are sending shoots

118

upward through the ground. Before long, spring and summer, with their colorful flowers and fresh green grass, will come virtually simultaneously. In the autumn, red dragonflies will dart through the clear air, and the cows will be seen returning to the barns.

I am certain that in this great gardenlike natural environment, the kindergarten children will grow and develop exactly in accordance with the school motto: "Strong, Correct and Sound." The more contact I have with these children, the more sure I become that they are fully capable of growing up into proud princes and princesses.

By coincidence, on the day of the opening of our kindergarten, on a highland in the Hitsujigaoka hills, an unveiling ceremony was held for a statue of William S. Clark, an American educator who played an important role in the development of Hokkaido in the late nineteenth century. Seeing this statue, I realized again that, in all historical periods, educators must be selfless.

Before the ceremonies started, I went to the entrance hall to await and greet eagerly the children who were arriving with their parents. I wanted to give myself entirely to welcoming these emissaries from the future. As I took each hand and embraced each child, I felt I respected and trusted them all. I seemed to see the bright light of the Japan and

the world of the future deep in their eyes. In congratulating them I said I hoped they would accept the responsibility for the twenty-first century.

I wonder why the axiom that good stock is necessary to produce good trees remains forgotten. Everyone talks of the crimes of youth and the impoverishment of education. Parents who are with children day in, day out must feel great nervousness and impatience. I understand that the educational executive system entails mountainous problems. But revolutions in executive policies alone will not facilitate the unravelling of the difficulties.

The term *educational industry* is not merely empty irony. To a startling extent, education has actually been converted into economic enterprise. This suggests an aspect of overall commercialism in modern society. An age in which education is treated as a means to an end can only be called nightmarish. I have always insisted on and followed a course dedicated to protecting the independence of learning and of the right to education. The range of human education can be described as the future itself. No matter how it dashes along, it has no ultimate goal. My two predecessors as president of Soka Gakkai have dealt with this difficult undertaking, which demands both perseverance and enduring power. And they have passed the baton to me. On the occasion of the opening of this institution, which marks the completion of our education system from kindergarten to university, I have allowed myself to speak on controversial topics. Please disregard it.

During this trip to Hokkaido I took my first ride on a school bus. I made two trips until all of the children were delivered to their front doors. The bus was a bustling paradise of modern-day children.

One of them said, "Mr. Ikeda, let's play guessing games. What has big wings and goes up and down?" When I replied, "A butterfly," all of them shouted in chorus, "Right!"

Children have an inexhaustible store of things to talk about. They think and think and in complete sincerity talk in the world of the imagination. Trying to get a firm hold on the world of dreams, one of them said, "The day will come when robots fly and go round and round the earth. Won't it?" Suddenly another one asked, "Mr. Ikeda, you've been to lots of places. You've been to France, haven't you?" I answered, "Yes, I have. Next time, let's all go together. All right?"

They said, "Yes. And will you come on one of our school outings too?" I promised that I would.

Given an opportunity to exchange views with these dwellers in an unpretentious, unhesitating, liberated world, I felt purified. Still I realized that an adult must educate himself carefully if he wants to keep up with children.

As I left the gentle Hitsujigaoka hills, I thought of Friedrich Froebel [1782–1852], the German educator and founder of the kindergarten system. In his autobiography, Froebel tells how on a spring day in 1840, as he was climbing a hill overlooking the town of Blankenburg and was, as usual, engrossed in thoughts of child education, he got the idea for the kindergarten. The story goes that, as he stood on the hill in the sunset, the town below looked like a huge garden. Suddenly he realized that a garden for children was what he wanted his school to be. Filled with joy, he dashed down the hill. And this is supposed to be the explanation for the word *kindergarten*.

This great educator loved children deeply and joined in their laughter, singing and playing to the extent that the local citizens ridiculed him as foolish. His educational motto advised adults to try to enter into the lives of children.

His book on human education, *The Education of Man* (*Die Menschenerziehung*), is regarded as a classic. The spirit of his motto sets forth exhaustively all the things that educators ought to be. It breaks away from abstractions and tells the prospective teacher that he must walk right beside the young children and live in close companionship with them all the time. If children are compared with plants and flowers in the kindergarten, the teachers are the gardeners who must care for and protect them.

I have heard you too are deeply concerned about children and the future of education and devote much thought to these issues. In books like *Shirobamba*, *Natsu kusa fuyu nami* (Summer grasses, winter waves) and *Asunaro monogatari*, I sense a smell of grassy fields that probably filled the youth of Yasushi Inoue. I was deeply impressed by one of the installments of your serial *Osanakihi no koto* (Of the days of youth), which appeared in the *Mainichi Shimbun*. In it you described the happiness of living gently embraced and protected. A young boy who has parted from his parents lives in the garden of nature. He breathes the aroma of fresh spring grass and the sultry smells of the summer fields. In autumn he walks on crackling fallen leaves and, in winter, endures the sharp, cold winds. Though I may be overstepping the amateur's bounds, I should like to believe that your lyrical descriptions of nature are based on experiences from your childhood. In my eyes, the boy in the blue, straight-sleeved kimono and straw sandals walking the Shimoda road at sunset, enticed homeward by the smell of cooking food, overlaps with Yasushi Inoue of today, who has traveled and written about the Silk Road and the ways of Alexander and the Romans. I suspect those childhood days are an important part of the total picture.

Froebel says that by the age of five a child has already learned all he needs to know for the rest of his life. Perhaps I am being audacious in applying them to you, but these meaningful words strike a cord that seems in harmony with your writing.

Some psychologists say that after the stage of childhood human beings pass into what is called the season of humanization. (In a sense, of course, all of human life could be called the season of humanization.)

In an age when reexaminations are being made of the ways in which we can live in keeping with the best of human nature, the significance of the season of humanization to children deserves thought. This might seem to be pursuing the issue the long way around, but I suspect it may be a short cut to truth about humanity.

For instance, just as multiplicity and variety distinguish the lives of adults, so each child has his own world. Examining these worlds from a lofty adult standpoint can lead only to criticism. It is important to try to put oneself in the child's place, to discover his dimension of thought and to learn what causes him suffering. Carrying out the frequently voiced admonition to put oneself in the other's shoes actually demands tremendous effort. The extent to which the adult is able to enter the child's mind is the first clue to ways to help the child's true qualities to emerge and come to full bloom.

In order to evoke the creativity of children, Froebel made their immaturity his immaturity and made their liveliness a detonating force in his own life. I discover something miraculous in the forward-looking figure of the educator who has given his whole soul to his task.

The season of humanization is the most beautiful time in the life of

children, probably because it is the time when they begin to emit the glow of truly human sentiments. They start reacting to the beauty of nature. They are sensitively moved by the worlds of small animals and plants. They begin to take the part of the small and abused when older, mischievous children pick on their juniors. For the first times in their lives, such treasures of the human heart as warm, private confidences and exchanges among companions and friends become important.

Experiences of this kind teach children the unlimited possibilities inherent in human beings. These possibilities are nurtured equally without being lost because the lives of young people are in early vigorous stages. I have limitless trust and wholehearted faith in these aspects of youth.

Beginning with the intention of reporting to you about the opening of our Sapporo kindergarten, I have let my pen ramble. I wanted to talk in detail about your work on Sen no Rikyū but instead have concentrated only on my own interests. Please forgive me.

For me too April, the month of the cherry trees, is unforgettable. My mentor Jōsei Toda, of whom I have spoken on other occasions, died on April 2. Each year on this day I renew my determination in connection with our mission. I am grateful to have such a day of remembrance and tension. Because of it, when the cherries have bloomed and fallen, I am ready to progress with new vigor.

On April 25 of this year, our organization's newspaper, the *Seikyō Shimbun*, celebrates its twenty-fifth anniversary. In connection with the occasion, I have written, "A newspaper is new each day, but this does not mean that it should pursue no more than novelty. The age demands expansion from scoop to scope." Our year's correspondence has helped me broaden my scope. I am grateful that you, a careful literary artist, have openly shared your thoughts with me in this form. Both the controlled elegance of your style and the experiences you have described impressed me deeply. In grateful conclusion, I extend my wish that you will care for yourself well and remain in good health for the sake of literature and humanity.

Daisaku Ikeda